C. W. Warden

# Alphabetical code of signals

For the use of Government pilot, surveying, light, buoy and other vessels,

telegraph stations, etc.

C. W. Warden

**Alphabetical code of signals**
*For the use of Government pilot, surveying, light, buoy and other vessels, telegraph stations, etc.*

ISBN/EAN: 9783741133916

Manufactured in Europe, USA, Canada, Australia, Japa

Cover: Foto ©Thomas Meinert / pixelio.de

Manufactured and distributed by brebook publishing software
(www.brebook.com)

C. W. Warden

**Alphabetical code of signals**

By Authority.

# ALPHABETICAL CODE OF SIGNALS

FOR THE USE OF

GOVERNMENT PILOT, SURVEYING, LIGHT, BUOY, AND
OTHER VESSELS, TELEGRAPH STATIONS, &c.

**COMPILED BY C. W. WARDEN.**

**SECOND EDITION.**

CALCUTTA:

OFFICE OF SUPERINTENDENT OF GOVERNMENT PRINTING.

1868.

# CONTENTS.

# CONTENTS.

## PART V—*Continued.*

# Pilot's Code

| | | |
|---|---|---|
| East India Jack | Code Signal and Interrogative Flag. | Compass Signal |
| B | C | D | F |
| G | H | J | K |
| L | M | N | P |
| Q | R | S Telegraph | T Rendezvous. |
| V | W Service Pendent | Assent. | Negative. |
| Answering | Master Attendant. | Senior Branch. | Senior Cruising. |

Pilots' Code

# Marryatt's Code.

# PREFACE TO THE SECOND EDITION.

FIVE years have elapsed since the present system of signalizing was introduced, and the Compiler trusts that it has been found to have many advantages over the old plan of numerals.

In the edition of 1845,—in which the Flags used were in numerals,—the sentences in Part V number one thousand and eighty-three—nine of which could only be made with one Flag, eighty-one with two Flags, six hundred and thirty with three Flags, when a fourth Flag was obliged to be used : whereas by the present system of letters, the following facts show a decided improvement.

In the first edition of the present Code, there were three hundred and twenty-one more sentences than in that of 1845, and the advantages of signalizing over the old plan are as follow :—Eighteen signals can be made with one Flag, three hundred and six with two Flags, and the remainder—consisting of one thousand and ninety-eight sentences—can be shown with three. In this edition there are some three or four hundred more sentences requiring only three Flags.

In the present edition *Marryatt's Flags only are used*, but have been so arranged, that it is not possible for a sentence in the Pilot's Code to be *made*, which, on looking into Marryatt's Signal Book, could convey any sense in its purport; there is therefore no possibility of confusion.

The Compiler begs to tender his warmest acknowledgments to those who have rendered him material assistance in the compilation of this Work.

# EXPLANATION OF PARTS OF CODE.

## PART I.

Distinguished in the Pilot's Code by the Service Pendant over letter.

Distinguished in Marryatt's Code, as painted in the Book, by Marryatt's 4th Pendant over Marryatt's Flags corresponding to the letter as placed in Marryatt's Code; the Service Pendant will not be seen as the Upper Flag in any other part of this Code.

## PART II.

Distinguished by the East India Jack over letter in the Pilot's Code and the White Flag *underneath* the letter in Marryatt's Code.

## PART III.

Distinguished in Pilot's Code by the Buoy Flag over letter.

Distinguished in Marryatt's Code by Ensign over letter.

This Flag, which is letter V, will not be seen as the Upper Flag in any other part of this Code.

## PART IV.

Distinguished in Pilot's Code by the Rendezvous over letter.

Distinguished in Marryatt's Code by the Rendezvous Flag over letter.   The letter T will not be seen as an Upper Flag in any other part of this Code.

## PART V.

Shows no distinguishing Flag in either Code; the letters T, V, and W will not be seen as Upper Flags in this part of the Code.

## PART VI.

Distinguished by Compass Signal over letter in both Codes.

## PART VII.

### NIGHT SIGNALS.

# PROPER USING OF THIS CODE.

## I.

When Pilots of Merchant Vessels are desirous of signalizing with each other in this Code, the following plan is in every case to be adopted : The vessel's number is to be made with whom the party wishes to signalize, *and the White Flag shown underneath the number;* this will show to the Pilot of the ship whose number is made that the Pilot's Code is about to be used.

## II.

When Pilots of Merchant Vessels are desirous of signalizing with Government Vessels, *the White Flag is to be shown underneath* the letter, corresponding to the vessel's name in *Marryatt's Code.*

## III.

When Pilots of Merchant Vessels are desirous of signalizing with Lighthouses or Telegraph Stations, the Rendezvous Flag over letter in *Marryatt's Code* is to be used, *White Flag underneath ;* this will show to the man in charge of such Lighthouse or Telegraph Station that the Pilot's Code is to be used.

## IV.

When Government Vessels wish to signalize with each other using this Code, *are in every case first to hoist the*

*Code Signal;* on this being answered, both parties are to understand that the Pilot's Code is to be used.

### V.

Should a Merchant Ship not have Marryatt's Pendant (4) on board, and the Pilot of such vessel carries a Private Flag, it can be used to take the place of letter W., *so that any Flag not in the Marryatt's Code, seen in any signal, it is to be understood as meaning letter W. in Marryatt's Code or Pilot's Private Flag.*

### VI.

When Government Pilot Vessels signalize the number of each grade, the following plan is to be adopted :—

If only Branch Pilots are on board, the signal showing the number is to be hoisted as heretofore.

When both Branch and Brevet Branches, the Answering Pendant shown between two Flags denotes the Upper Flag as Branch, the Lower as Brevet Branch. When only Brevet Branches are on board, the Answering Pendant is shown underneath a Flag.

When signalizing the number of Masters on board, in order to distinguish Senior from Junior, the following plan is to be adopted :—

If any Senior Masters, the number will be hoisted as heretofore.

If both Seniors and Juniors, the Second distinguishing Pendant is to be used in a similar manner as the Answering Pendant in the case of Branch Pilots.

In signalizing the number of Mates, the third Pendant is to be shown as in that for Masters.

## VII.

All depths of water will be signalized reduced to zero in feet by the Numeral Flags of Marryatt's Code, with Marryatt's Numeral Pendant over.

All distances will in like manner be signalized in yards.

## VIII.

Pilot Vessels attending distressed ships will on sighting a Red Buoy hoist Buoy Flag at Main; on sighting a Black Buoy, Buoy Flag at Fore; on seeing two Buoys at the same time on opposite sides of the Channel, the Buoy Flag at Main will denote a Western Flag, and the Red Flag at Fore an Eastern one.

## IX.

Buoy Vessels when laying a Western Buoy, will show at Main a Red Flag.

When laying an Eastern Buoy, will show at Main a Blue Flag.

When laying a Wreck Buoy, will show at Main a Buoy Flag.

When laying a Fair Way Buoy, will show at Main a Buoy Flag.

## X.

The Interrogative Flag, when shown over a signal, will give the sentence an interrogative character, and in the case of such signal being made by a Junior to a Senior Officer, is also to be considered as asking permission to carry out the purport of the signal.

### XI.

Each part of the present Code will have blank place where the subject finishes for the purpose of entering any additional matter, when the sanction of competent authority has been obtained.

### XII.

The Fourth Pendant Marryatt's, in Marryatt's Code, takes the place of the Private Flag in the present Code letter W, there was no other plan to be adopted, unless every running Pilot carried a Private Flag; in such a case the Private Flag could have taken the place of the Fourth Pendant, but as such is not the case, and the Code would be incomplete without a Flag, nothing else can be done.

When wishing to signalize the number of Officers on board, depth of water, or any signals where numerals are required, the old system is to be adopted, commencing from letter G, in both Codes which represents No. 1, and so on till R, which represents 0.

During the time the Compiler is a member of the Service, Part I will be corrected at the commencement of every succeeding year, and any necessary sentences added to Parts II, III, IV, V, as may be deemed necessary in order to keep the Code as perfect as possible.

### XIII.

When the Master Attendant or Deputy Master Attendant are afloat, the vessel they are on board of will carry his Flag at the Main. When any of the Assistants are on board, his Flag will be shown at the Fore.

# ADDENDA.

In Clause IV of the General Instructions it is to be always understood that Government Vessels *make the numbers* of the Vessel they wish to signalize to *before hoisting* the Code Signal.

Government Vessels wishing to signalize with Merchant Vessels will in all cases make the Vessel's number they signalize to with a white flag underneath; this will show the Pilots' Code is to be used.

Government Vessels wishing to signalize to Lighthouses, Light Vessels, Signal or Telegraph Stations, will adopt the same plan as is mentioned in Clause I of Addenda.

Lighthouses, Light Vessels, Signal or Telegraph Stations wishing to signalize with Merchant Vessels, will make the Vessel's number in Marryatt's Code, white flag underneath.

Lighthouses, Light Vessels, Signal or Telegraph Stations wishing to signalize with Government Vessels, will adopt the same plan as is mentioned in Clause I of Addenda.

It now only remains to mention the reason for transposing the flags in Marryatt's Code, as has been done in order to make two distinct Codes with one set of flags.

Supposing a Pilot Vessel wishes to signalize the number of Officers on board, and this number happens to be as follows :—

> *Viz.,* one Branch, one Brevet Branch.
>    „   Senior Master, one Junior Master.
>    „   Senior Mate, one Junior Mate.

From the above it will be seen that six flags are required, and, to make this signal with one hoist, it would require three distinct Codes; as six flags are to be hoisted all together and all meaning the numeral one, therefore, if the flags in the Pilots' Code had been placed exactly in the same manner as those in Marryatt's Code, these signals could not have been made but with one hoist; this would have been No. 1, and the white flag underneath the answering Pendant, which repeats the numeral of the upper flag.

In order, therefore, to avoid any confusion, should it be found requisite to make such a signal as the one given, the following rule will answer :—

One Branch and one Brevet Branch, distinguished by No. 1 and No. 4 Marryatt's, with answering Pendant between, at the Peak.

One Senior Master and one Junior Master with No. 1 and No. 4 Marryatt's, with second Pendant between, at the Main.

One Senior Mate and one Junior Mate, the 4th Distinguishing Pendant Marryatt's and White Flags, with third Pendant Marryatt's between, at the fore, so that with two sets of flags, all these signals can be made with one hoist; it is therefore to be distinctly understood that when showing the number of Officers, the fourth Pendant in Marryatt's Code hoisted at the fore or an upper flag conveys the same meaning in number as the upper flag, at the Main and Peak, when not hoisted singly.

# RIVER SURVEYORS' SIGNALS.

## I.

A large Blue Flag over a signal when shown from any of the Surveying Vessels, or from any Telegraph Station, denote such signal to be from River Surveyor.

## II.

All signals referring to names and position of Buoys, will be made from Part III of Pilot's Code.

## III.

All signals referring to names of places and river marks will, in like manner, be made from Part IV of Pilot's Code.

## IV.

When the Telegraph Flag in Marryatt's is seen next below the Blue Flag, the signal is a sentence, and will be found at each end of the sentences placed alphabetically.

## V.

The Compass Signals will be made as in Part V of Pilot's Code.

## VI.

All depths of water will be signalized reduced to zero in feet by the Numeral Flags of Marryatt's Code, with Marryatt's Numeral Pendant over.

## VII.

All distances will be in like manner shown in yards.

B

## VIII.

All description of vessels, whether Government or Merchant, when within signal distance of any of the Surveying Vessels, or of any Telegraph Station in any part of the river, observe flying on board of any such vessel, or at any such Telegraph Station, a large Blue Flag over a signal, such signal is to be noticed and the purport of it to be acted upon, as all such signals will refer to changes in the Channels, changes in the positions of Buoys, changes in the colours of Buoys, changes in the depth of water, or any other information important to the safe navigation of vessels.

## IX.

Signals from River Surveyor to vessels passing up and down will be found at the end of, and separate from, Parts III, IV, and V placed alphabetically.

# PART I.

## PRINCIPAL OFFICERS OF THE STATE,

ALSO

## PILOT SERVICE.

Distinguished in Pilot's Code by the Service Pendant over the Flags.

Distinguished in Marryatt's Code by Marryatt's 4th Pendant over the Flags.

# PART I.

## Service Pendant over Letter.

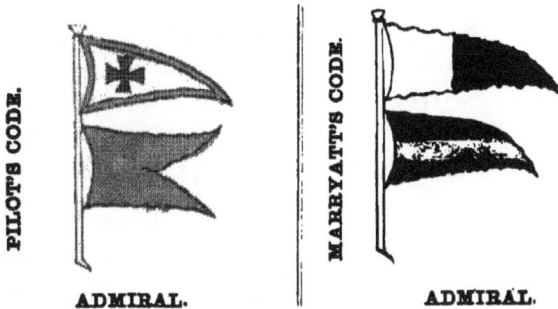

PILOT'S CODE.

MARRYATT'S CODE.

ADMIRAL.

ADMIRAL.

## PRINCIPAL OFFICERS OF THE STATE.

| Letters. | Designation. |
|----------|--------------|
| B | Viceroy and Governor General. |
| C | Governor of Madras. |
| D | Governor of Bombay. |
| F | Governor, Lieutenant, of Bengal. |
| G | Governor, Lieutenant, of North-West Provinces. |
| H | President of Council. |
| J | Justice, Chief. |
| K | Bishop. |
| L | Commander-in-Chief. |
| M | Admiral. |
| N | Commodore. |
| P | Member of Council. |
| Q | Judge, Puisne. |
| R | Commissioner of Police. |
| S | Secretary to Government. |
| T | Master Attendant. |
| V | |

## PILOT SERVICE.

### Service Pendant over Letter.

*1875*

| LETTERS. | Names | LETTERS. | Names |
|---|---|---|---|
| B C | C. ... ... | C B | ... ... ... |
| B D | C. B. Youngs | C D | F. Dyer |
| B F | C. C. Smythe | C F | J. Barnett |
| B G | R. B. Yates | C G | W. O. West |
| B H | R. M. Daly | C H | W. K. Douglas |
| B J | C. Nelson | C J | F. Ancell |
| B K | R. W. Long | C K | J. H. Lambrick |
| B L | A. E. Milner | C L | D. J. Scott |
| B M | R. S. Evans | C M | W. A. Symons |
| B N | C. Harrell | C N | B. Mauger |
| B P | J. D. Osborne | C P | J. Syverett |
| B Q | O. Nash | C Q | J. Doggett |
| B R | R. C. Rutherford | C R | R. Rust |
| B S | J. H. Wells | C S | C. Collingwood |
| B T | J. Taylor | C T | S. Ransom |
| B V | W. H. Simpkins | C V | H. Jones |

# PART I.

## PILOT SERVICE.

### Service Pendant over Letter.

| Letters. | Names | Letters. | Names |
|---|---|---|---|
| D B | D. F. Miller | F B | S. E. Walker. |
| D C | J. Sherman | F C | H. Lindquist |
| D F | C. S. Mills | F D | R. J. Mowle. |
| D G | G. Anderson | F G | J. Raijus |
| D H | S. R. Elson | F H | G. Burn |
| D J | W. Woolridge | F J | N. Wann |
| D K | A Hough | F K | J. Christie |
| D L | J. Collingwood | F L | P. J. Holt |
| D M | M. McCaskill | F M | J. B. Ramsay |
| D N | A. W. Phipson | F N | G. J. Smeart |
| D P | E. Hudson | F P | F. C. Cooper |
| D Q | J. F. Broadhead. | F Q | L. P. Goodwyn |
| D R | J. S. Simons | F R | C. A. Lidstone |
| D S | J. Peddie | F S | S. Bartlett |
| D T | E. J. Rayner | F T | P. Poulson |
| D V | R. A Wortley | F V | W. Hart |

# PART I.

## PILOT SERVICE.

### Service Pendant over Letter.

| Letters. | Names | Letters. | Names. |
|---|---|---|---|
| G B | F. D. Bellew | H B | A. Fuller. |
| G C | W. A. Scaly | H C | A. W. Phipson, |
| G D | C. Williams | H D | A. M. Merriott. |
| G F | J. D. Bonnell | H F | H. Steans. |
| G H | A. Rinauland | H G | J. Baxter. |
| G J | W. Laws. | H J | E. F. Hudson. |
| G K | F. Doyle | H K | J. F. Broadhead. |
| G L | H. Coker | H L | J. L. Simons. |
| G M | R. Shelverton | H M | F. Reddie. |
| G N | F. C. Sparling | H N | F. T. Rayner. |
| G P | W. G. Connolly | H P | F. E. Huggett. |
| G Q | W. Kendai. | H Q | W. Rudd. X |
| G R | | H R | W. D. Bristow. X |
| G S | | H S | H. Browne. x |
| G T | | H T | R. A. Wortley. |
| G V | | H V | S. E. Walker. |

# PART I.

## PILOT SERVICE.

### Service Pendant over Letter.

| Letters. | Names. | Letters. | Names. |
|---|---|---|---|
| J B | J. W. Terry. ✗ | K B | S. D. O. Walters. |
| J C | H. Lindquist. | K C | S. Bartlett. |
| J D | R. J. Mowle. | K D | J. D. Hough. |
| J F | J. Ralph. | K F | A. A. Madden. |
| J G | G. Burn. | K G | R. G. Hand. ✗ |
| J H | W. Thompson. ✗ | K H | W. R. Williams. |
| J K | N. T. Wawn. | K J | P. J. Holt. |
| J L | S. J. Tucker. ✗ | K L | W. H. Bradley. ✗ |
| J M | W. Thomson. | K M | J. B. Ramsay. |
| J N | H. J. Cox. | K N | G. Chitty. ✗ |
| J P | E. C. Kemp. ✗ | K P | J. H. Elson. ✗ |
| J Q | W. Bowden. | K Q | H. E. Miller. ✗ |
| J R | N. M. Wall. | K R | G. J. C. Smart. |
| J S | J. Ewart. ✗ | K S | F. C. Cooper. |
| J T | P. E. LeCouteur. | K T | L. P. Goodwyn. |
| J V | J. Christie. | K V | A. Templeton. |

# PART I.

## PILOT SERVICE.

### Service Pendant over Letter.

| LETTERS. | NAMES. | LETTERS. | NAMES. |
|---|---|---|---|
| L B | P. Paulson. | M B | R. H. Shelverton. |
| L C | W. Hart. | M C | J. F. Chadwick. ✕ |
| L D | R. Scott. | M D | G. A. Wright. ✕ |
| L F | F. D. Bellew. | M F | E. Huey. ✕ |
| L G | W. Morgan. | M G | |
| L H | F. H. W. Wright. | M H | |
| L J | W. A. Sealy. | M J | |
| L K | C. Williams. | M K | |
| L M | W. E. Jackson. | M L | |
| L N | C. A. Lidstone. | M N | |
| L P | J. D. Bennett. | M P | |
| L Q | F. C. LeBreton. ✕ | M Q | |
| L R | A. Renauland. | M R | |
| L S | F. Doyle. | M S | |
| L T | F. H. Robilliard. ✕ | M T | |
| L V | H. Coker. | M V | |

# PART I.

## PILOT SERVICE.

### Service Pendant over Letter.

| Letters. | Names. | Letters. | Names. |
|---|---|---|---|
| N B | | P B | |
| N C | | P C | |
| N D | | P D | |
| N F | | P F | |
| N G | | P G | |
| N H | | P H | |
| N J | | P J | |
| N K | | P K | |
| N L | | P L | |
| N M | | P M | |
| N P | | P N | |
| N Q | | P Q | |
| N R | | P R | |
| N S | | P S | |
| N T | | P T | |
| N V | | P V | |

# PART II.

## GOVERNMENT VESSELS.

Distinguished in Pilot's Code by East India Jack over
the Flags.

Distinguished in Marryatt's Code by Compass Flag
underneath the Flags.

## GOVERNMENT VESSELS.

### East India Jack over Letter.

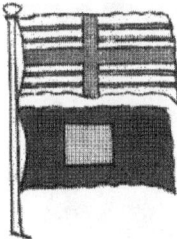

FAME S. V. (Pilot's Code)

FAME S. V. (Marryatt's Code)

| LETTERS. | NAMES OF VESSELS. | LETTERS. | | NAMES OF VESSELS. |
|---|---|---|---|---|
| B | Feroze. ✗ | B | C | |
| C | | B | D | Arracan. ✗ |
| D | Cassandra. | B | F | Prince Arthur. ✗ |
| F | Kedgree. | B | G | Undaunted. |
| G | Chinsurah. | B | H | Celerity. |
| H | Foam. | B | J | Proserpine. |
| J | Guide. | B | K | Nemesis. |
| K | Fame. | B | L | Pluto. |
| L | Marie. | B | M | Czarewitch. |
| M | Grappler. | B | N | Qwan Tung. |
| N | | B | P | Agitator. |
| P | Comet. | B | Q | Dolphin. |
| Q | Star. | B | R | |
| R | Mutlah. | B | S | |
| S | Deva. | B | T | |
| T | Saugor. | B | V | |
| V | Megna. | B | W | |
| W | | C | B | |

# PART III.

## NAMES OF BUOYS.

Distinguished in Pilot's Code by Buoy Flag over the
Flags.

Distinguishde in Marryatt's Code by Ship's Ensign
over the Flags.

D

# NAMES OF BUOYS.

## Buoy Flag over Letter.

PILOT'S CODE.

MARRYATT'S CODE.

PILOT'S RIDGE BUOY.          PILOT'S RIDGE BUOY.

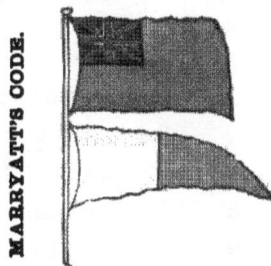

| Letters. | Names of Buoys. |
|---|---|
| B | False Point Anchoring Buoy A. |
| C | False Point Anchoring Buoy B. |
| D | False Point Anchoring Buoy C. |
| F | False Point Anchoring Buoy D. |
| G | Kanaka Buoy. |
| H | Dumrah River Anchoring Buoy. |
| J | Dumrah River Fair Way Buoy. |
| K | Dumrah River North Bank Buoy I. |
| L | Dumrah River North Bank Buoy II. |
| M | Dumrah River North Bank Buoy III. |
| N | Dumrah River North Bank Buoy IV. |
| P | Dumrah River North Bank Buoy V. |
| Q | Dumrah River South Bank Buoy I. |
| R | Dumrah River South Bank Buoy II. |
| S | Dumrah River South Bank Buoy III. |
| T | |
| W | Pilot's Ridge Buoy. |

# PART III.

## NAMES OF BUOYS.

### Buoy Flag over Letter.

| LETTERS. | NAMES OF BUOYS. |
|---|---|
| B C | Balasore Anchoring Buoy. |
| B D | Balasore Bar Buoy. |
| B F | Western Reef Buoy. |
| B G | Western Channel Reef Buoy. |
| B H | Western Channel Spit Buoy. |
| B J | Western Channel Lower Middle Ground Buoy. |
| B K | Western Channel Centre Middle Ground Buoy. |
| B L | Western Channel Upper Middle Ground Buoy. |
| B M | Eagle Channel L Buoy. |
| B N | Eagle Channel K Buoy. |
| B P | Eagle Channel J Buoy. |
| B Q | Eagle Channel H Buoy. |
| B R | Eagle Channel G Buoy. |
| B S | Eagle Channel F Buoy. |
| B T | Eagle Channel E Buoy. |
| B W | Eagle Channel D Buoy. |

# PART III.

## NAMES OF BUOYS.

### Buoy Flag over Letter.

| LETTERS. | NAMES OF BUOYS. |
|---|---|
| C B | Eagle Channel C Buoy. |
| C D | Eagle Channel B Buoy. |
| C F | Eagle Channel A Buoy. |
| C G | Eastern Channel Floating Light Buoy. |
| C H. | Eastern Channel Lower Reef Buoy. |
| C J | Eastern Channel Upper Reef Buoy. |
| C K | Eastern Channel Lower Middle Ground Buoy. |
| C L | Eastern Channel Upper Middle Ground Buoy. |
| C M | Saugor Sand Lower Buoy. |
| C N | Saugor Sand Centre Buoy. |
| C P | Saugor Sand Upper Buoy. |
| C Q | Thornhills' Channel Fair Way Buoy. |
| C R | Reef Head Passage Lower Eastern Buoy. |
| C S | Reef Head Passage Lower Western Buoy. |
| C T | Reef Head Passage Upper Eastern Buoy. |
| C W | Reef Head Passage Upper Western Buoy. |

# PART III.

## NAMES OF BUOYS.

### Buoy Flag over Letter.

| Letters. | Names of Buoys. |
|---|---|
| D B | Reef Head Buoy. |
| D C | Thornhills' Channel Lower Eastern Buoy. |
| D F | Thornhills' Channel Lower Western or Anchoring Buoy. |
| D G | Thornhills' Channel Centre Eastern Buoy. |
| D H | Thornhills' Channel Centre Western Buoy. |
| D J | Thornhills' Channel Upper Eastern Buoy. |
| D K | Thornhills' Channel Upper Western Buoy. |
| D L | Gasper Channel Lower Eastern Buoy. |
| D M | Gasper Channel Lower Western Buoy. |
| D N | Gasper Channel Centre Eastern Buoy. |
| D P | Gasper Channel Centre Western Buoy. |
| D Q | Gasper Channel Upper Eastern Buoy. |
| D R | Gasper Channel Upper Western Buoy. |
| D S | Western Brace Buoy. |
| D T | Solah Buoy. |
| D W | Eastern Brace Buoy. |

# PART III.

## NAMES OF BUOYS.

### Buoy Flag over Letter.

| LETTERS. | NAMES OF BUOYS. |
|---|---|
| F B | Mizen Buoy. |
| F C | Saugor Anchoring Buoy. |
| F D | Long Sand Spit Buoy. |
| F G | Lloyd's Channel Lower, Western Buoy. |
| F H | Saugor Flat Lower Western Buoy. |
| F J | Saugor Flat Centre Western Buoy. |
| F K | Saugor Flat Upper Western Buoy. |
| F L | Bedford's Channel Lower Western Buoy. |
| F M | Bedford's Channel Centre Western Buoy. |
| F N | Bedford's Channel Upper Western Buoy. |
| F P | Bedford's Channel Lower Eastern Buoy. |
| F Q | Bedford's Channel Upper Eastern Buoy. |
| F R | Dredge Channel Lower Western Buoy. |
| F S | Dredge Channel Upper Western Buoy. |
| F T | Dredge Channel Lower Eastern Buoy. |
| F W | Dredge Channel Centre Eastern Buoy. |

# PART III.

## NAMES OF BUOYS.

### Buoy Flag over Letter.

| Letters. | Names of Buoys. |
|---|---|
| G B | Dredge Channel Upper Eastern Buoy. |
| C C | Auckland Channel Lower Western Buoy. |
| C D | Auckland Channel Lower Eastern Buoy. |
| G F | Auckland Channel Upper Western Buoy. |
| G H | Auckland Channel Upper Eastern Buoy. |
| G J | |
| G K | Mud Point Channel Lower Western Buoy. |
| G L | Mud Point Channel Lower Eastern Buoy. |
| G M | Mud Point Channel Centre Western Buoy. |
| G N | Mud Point Channel Centre Eastern Buoy. |
| G P | Mud Point Channel Upper Western Buoy. |
| G Q | Mud Point Channel Upper Eastern Buoy. |
| G R | Jellingham Channel Lower Western Buoy. |
| G S | Jellingham Channel Lower Eastern Buoy. |
| G T | Jellingham Channel Centre Western Buoy. |
| G W | Jellingham Channel Centre Eastern Buoy. |

# PART III.

## NAMES OF BUOYS.

### Buoy Flag over Letter.

| LETTERS. | NAMES OF BUOYS. |
|---|---|
| H B | Jellingham Channel Upper Western Buoy. |
| H C | Jellingham Channel Upper Eastern Buoy. |
| H D | Channel Creek Lower Buoy. |
| H F | Channel Creek Centre Buoy. |
| H G | Channel Creek Upper Buoy. |
| H J | Rangafulla Lower Buoy      *(L. R.)* |
| H K | Rangafulla Middle Buoy     *(M. R.)* |
| H L | Outer Rangafulla Channel Lower Western Buoy. |
| H M | Outer Rangafulla Channel Lower Eastern Buoy. |
| H N | Outer Rangafulla Channel Centre Western Buoy. |
| H P | Outer Rangafulla Channel Centre Eastern Buoy. |
| H Q | Outer Rangafulla Channel Upper Western Buoy. |
| H R | Outer Rangafulla Channel Upper Eastern Buoy. |
| H S | Centre Rangafulla Channel Lower Western Buoy. |
| H T | Centre Rangafulla Channel Lower Eastern Buoy. |
| H W | Centre Rangafulla Channel Centre Western Buoy. |

# PART III.

## NAMES OF BUOYS.

### Buoy Flag over Letter.

| Letters. | Names of Buoys. |
|---|---|
| J B | Centre Rangafulla Channel Centre Eastern Buoy. |
| J C | Centre Rangafulla Channel Upper Western Buoy. |
| J D | Centre Rangafulla Channel Upper Eastern Buoy. |
| J F | Silver Tree Channel Fair Way Buoy. |
| J G | Inner Rangafulla Channel Lower Western Buoy. |
| J H | Inner Rangafulla Channel Centre Western Buoy. |
| J K | Inner Rangafulla Channel Upper Western Buoy. |
| J L | Kulpee Anchoring Buoy. |
| J M | Kulpee Lower Buoy |
| J N | Kulpee Upper Buoy |
| J P | Kulpee Flat Nun Buoy, Red. |
| J Q | Canterbury Flat Nun Buoy, Black. |
| J R | Waterloo Wreck Buoy. |
| J S | Muckreputta Lump Buoy. |
| J T | Fort Mornington Flat Buoy. |
| J W | Fultah Sand Buoy. |

# PART III.

## NAMES OF BUOYS.

### Buoy Flag over Letter.

| LETTERS. | NAMES OF BUOYS. |
|----------|-----------------|
| K B | Fultah Flat Buoy. |
| K C | Fultah Anchoring Buoy, *Nun Red.* |
| K D | Garden Reach Flat Buoy, *Nun Red.* |
| K F | College Sand Buoy. |
| K G | |
| K H | |
| K J | |
| K L | |
| K M | |
| K N | |
| K P | |
| K Q | |
| K R | |
| K S | |
| K T | |
| K W | |

# PART III.

## RIVER SURVEYOR'S SIGNALS.

### Blue Flag over Signal.

| PILOT'S CODE. | MARRYATT'S CODE. |
|---|---|
|  | 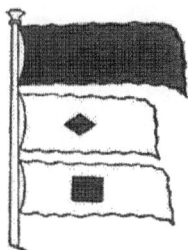 |
| UPPER EASTERN BUOY. | UPPER EASTERN BUOY. |

| LETTERS. | BUOYS, &c. |
|---|---|
| B | A Spire Buoy, Colour *as indicated*. |
| C | A Nun Buoy, Red. |
| D | A Nun Buoy, Black. |
| F | A Nun Buoy, White. |
| G | Buoy *as indicated* is in Shoal water. |
| H | Buoy *as indicated* has been moved, *direction indicated* by Compass Signal. |
| J | Buoy *as indicated* has been painted *as indicated*. |
| K | Buoy *as indicated* has been laid in Channel or off place indicated. |
| L | |
| M | |
| N | |
| P | |
| Q | Upper Eastern Buoy. |
| R | Upper Western Buoy. |
| S | Centre Eastern Buoy. • |
| T | Centre Western Buoy. |
| W | Lower Eastern Buoy. |

# PART III.

## RIVER SURVEYOR'S SIGNALS.

### Blue Flag over Signal.

| LETTERS. | BUOYS, &c. |
|---|---|
| B C | Lower Western Buoy. |
| B D | Fairway Buoy. |
| B F | Anchoring Buoy. |
| B G | Spit or Prong Buoy. |
| B H | Wreck Buoy. |
| B J | |
| B K | |
| B L | |
| B M | |
| B N | |
| B P | |
| B Q | |
| B R | |
| B S | |
| B T | |
| B W | |

# PART III.

## RIVER SURVEYOR'S SIGNALS.

### Blue Flag over Signal.

| Letters. | Buoys, &c. |
|---|---|
| C B | |
| C D | |
| C F | |
| C G | |
| C H | |
| C J | |
| C K | |
| C L | |
| C M | |
| C N | |
| C P | |
| C Q | |
| C R | |
| C S | |
| C T | |
| C W | |

# PART IV.

## NAMES OF PLACES, CREEKS, MARKS, &c.

### Distinguished in both of the Codes by Rendezvous Flag over Letter.

# PART IV.

## NAMES OF PLACES, CREEKS, MARKS, &c.

### Rendezvous Flag over Letter.

PILOT'S CODE.

MARRYATT'S CODE.

Wd. OF MARKS ON
ANCHORING CREEK RIDGE.

Wd. OF MARKS ON
ANCHORING CREEK RIDGE.

## RIVER SURVEYOR'S SIGNALS.

### Blue Flag over Rendezvous Flag.

PILOT'S CODE.

MARRYATT'S CODE.

Wd. OF MARKS ON
ANCHORING CREEK RIDGE.

Wd. OF MARKS ON
ANCHORING CREEK RIDGE.

# PART IV.

## NAMES OF PLACES, CREEKS, MARKS, &c.

### Rendezvous Flag over Letter.

| LETTERS. | NAMES. |
| --- | --- |
| B | Atcheepore E. T. Station. |
| C | Akra Farm House. |
| D | Anchoring Creek. |
| F | Anchoring Creek Ridge. |
| G | Anchoring Creek Ridge Track No. 1. |
| H | Anchoring Creek Ridge Track No. 2. |
| J | Anchoring Creek Ridge Track No. 3. |
| K | Anchoring Creek Ridge Marks on. |
| L | Anchoring Creek Ridge Wd. Marks on. |
| M | Anchoring Creek Obelisk. |
| N | Auckland Bar. |
| P | Auckland Channel. |
| Q | Balasore Flag Staff. |
| R | Balasore Hills. |
| S | Balasore River. |
| V | Balasore River Bar. |
| W | Balasore Roads. |

# PART IV.

## NAMES OF PLACES, CREEKS, MARKS, &c.

### Rendezvous Flag over Letter.

| Letters. | Names. |
|---|---|
| B C | Bamboo Grove. |
| B D | Bedford's Bar. |
| B F | Bedford's Channel. |
| B G | Bellary Semaphore Tower. |
| B H | Black Point. |
| B J | Bluff North. |
| B K | Bluff South. |
| B L | Brace Eastern. |
| B M | Brace Eastern, Head of. |
| B N | Brace Eastern, Tail of. |
| B P | Brace Eastern, Eastern edge of. |
| B Q | Brace Eastern, Western edge of. |
| B R | Brace Western. |
| B S | Brace Western, Head of. |
| B V | Brace Western, Tail of. |
| B W | Brace Western, Eastern edge of. |

# PART IV.

## NAMES OF PLACES, CREEKS, MARKS, &c.

### Rendezvous Flag over Letter.

| LETTERS. | NAMES. |
|---|---|
| C B | Brace Western, Western edge of. |
| C D | Brool Point. |
| C F | Brool Semaphore Tower. |
| C G | Budge-Budge. |
| C H | Budge-Budge Creek. |
| C J | Budge-Budge Flat. |
| C K | Budge-Budge House. |
| C L | Budge-Budge Reach. |
| C M | Budge-Budge Sand. |
| C N | Buffaloe Point. |
| C P | Caffray Point. |
| C Q | Caffray Reach. |
| C R | Caffray Sand. |
| C S | Calcutta Master Attendant's Office. |
| C V | Calcutta Harbour Master's Office. |
| C W | Calcutta Moorings. |

# PART IV.

## NAMES OF PLACES, CREEKS, MARKS, &c.

### Rendezvous Flag over Letter.

| LETTERS. | NAMES. |
|---|---|
| D B | Calcutta Reach. |
| D C | Camperbaches Point. |
| D F | Canterbury Point. |
| D G | Canterbury Flat. |
| D H | Canterbury Obelisk. |
| D J | Cassurina Bluff North. |
| D K | Cassurina Bluff South. |
| D L | Channel Creek. |
| D M | Channel Creek Sand. |
| D N | Channel Creek Lumps. |
| D P | Chingaree Creek. |
| D Q | Clumped Peak. |
| D R | College, Bishop's. |
| D S | College Sand. |
| D V | Cooley Depôt. |
| D W | Coverdales Bluff. |

# PART IV.

## NAMES OF PLACES, CREEKS, MARKS, &c.

### Rendezvous Flag over Letter.

| LETTERS. | NAMES. |
|---|---|
| F B | Cowcolly Light House. |
| F C | Cowcolly Roads. |
| F D | Cowcolly Beach. |
| F G | Damoodah River. |
| F H | Dariapore G. T. S. |
| F J | Deep Water Mark. |
| F K | Deep Water Point. |
| F L | Devil's Point. |
| F M | Dhaga Semaphore Tower. |
| F N | Diamond Harbour. |
| F P | Diamond Harbour Creek. |
| F Q | Diamond Harbour Custom House. |
| F R | Diamond Harbour E. T. Station. |
| F S | Diamond Harbour Flag Staff. |
| F V | Diamond Harbour Magistrate's House. |
| F W | Diamond Harbour Moorings. |

# PART IV.

## NAMES OF PLACES, CREEKS, MARKS, &c.

### Rendezvous Flag over Letter.

| Letters. | Names. |
| --- | --- |
| C B | Diamond Harbour Mud Battery. |
| C C | Diamond Point. |
| C D | Diamond Sand. |
| C F | Diamond Sand, Head of. |
| C H | Diamond Sand, Tail of. |
| C J | Diamond Sand, Spit of. |
| C K | Dog's Creek. |
| C L | Dodswell's Island. |
| C M | Double Tree Mark. |
| C N | Dredge Channel. |
| C P | Dredge Channel Anchorage. |
| C Q | Dumrah River. |
| C R | Dumrah River Bar. |
| C S | Dumrah River Beacon. |
| C V | Eagle Channel. |
| C W | Eagle Sand. |

# PART IV.

## NAMES OF PLACES, CREEKS, MARKS, &c.

### Rendezvous Flag over Letter.

| LETTERS. | NAMES. |
|---|---|
| H B | Eagle Sand, Head of. |
| H C | Eagle Sand, Tail of. |
| H D | Eagle Sand, Eastern edge of. |
| H F | Eagle Sand, Western edge of. |
| H G | Eastern Channel. |
| H J | Eastern Channel Light Station. |
| H K | False Point. |
| H L | False Point Anchorage. |
| H M | False Point Beacon. |
| H N | False Point Harbour. |
| H P | False Point Light House. |
| H Q | False Point Light House Creek. |
| H R | False Bay. |
| H S | Fisherman's Point. |
| H V | Fisherman's Point Anchorage. |
| H W | Fisherman's Flat. |

## NAMES OF PLACES, CREEKS, MARKS, &c.

### Rendezvous Flag over Letter.

| LETTERS. | NAMES. |
|---|---|
| J B | Floating Light Upper Gasper Channel. |
| J C | Floating Light Lower Gasper Channel. |
| J D | Floating Light Eastern Channel. |
| J F | Floating Light Pilot's Ridge. |
| J G | Fort Gloster Mills. |
| J H | Fort Gloster Point. |
| J K | Fort Gloster Flat. |
| J L | Fort Point. |
| J M | Fort Semaphore Tower. |
| J N | Fultah. |
| J P | Fultah Bight. |
| J Q | Fultah Creek. |
| J R | Fultah House. |
| J S | Fultah Point. |
| J V | Fultah Flat. |
| J W | Fultah Point Mark. |

# PART IV.

## NAMES OF PLACES, CREEKS, MARKS, &c.

### Rendezvous Flag over Letter.

| LETTERS. | NAMES. |
|---|---|
| K B | Fultah Point Old. |
| K C | Fultah Reach. |
| K D | Fultah Sand. |
| K F | Fultah Old. |
| K G | Fultah Old Point. |
| K H | Garden Reach. |
| K J | Garden House. |
| K L | Garden House Point. |
| K M | Gasper Channel. |
| K N | Gasper Channel Light Station. |
| K P | Gasper Sand, Head of. |
| K Q | Gasper Sand, Tail of. |
| K R | Gasper Sand, Eastern edge of. |
| K S | Gasper Sand, Western edge of. |
| K V | Gasper Sand. |
| K W | Gasper Sand between Prongs. |

# PART IV.

## NAMES OF PLACES, CREEKS, MARKS, &c.

### Rendezvous Flag over Letter.

| LETTERS. | NAMES. |
| --- | --- |
| L B | Gasper Sand Eastern Prong. |
| L C | Gasper Sand Western Prong. |
| L D | Gungra Semaphore Tower. |
| L F | Gungra G. T. S. |
| L G | Hangman's Point. |
| L H | Hastings. |
| L J | Hastings' Reach. |
| L K | Hastings' Moorings. |
| L M | Hastings' Bridge. |
| L N | Heerya Gunge Point. |
| L P | Hidgellee. |
| L Q | Hidgellee River. |
| L R | Hidgellee South Mark. |
| L S | Hidgellee Temple. |
| L V | Hidgellee Point. |
| L W | Hog River Creek. |

## NAMES OF PLACES, CREEKS, MARKS, &c.

### Rendezvous Flag over Letter.

| LETTERS. | NAMES. |
|---|---|
| M B | Hog River False Creek. |
| M C | Hog River Obelisk. |
| M D | Hog River Point. |
| M F | Hog River Reach. |
| M G | Hog River Sand. |
| M H | Hooghly Point. |
| M J | Hooghly Point Tidal Semaphore. |
| M K | Hooghly Point E. T. Station. |
| M L | Hooghly Point Index Piles. |
| M N | Hooghly Sand. |
| M P | Hooghly Sand, Back of. |
| M Q | Hooghly Sand, Head of. |
| M R | Hooghly Sand, Tail of. |
| M S | Hooghly Sand, Spit of. |
| M V | Hooghly Bight. |
| M W | Hoorungotta River. |

# PART IV.

## NAMES OF PLACES, CREEKS, MARKS, &c.

### Rendezvous Flag over Letter.

| Letters. | Names. |
|----------|--------|
| N B | Hope's Obelisk. |
| N C | Hospital Point. |
| N D | Hospital Creek. |
| N F | Hospital Flat. |
| N G | Huldea River. |
| N H | Huldea River Mark. |
| N J | Jack Straw's House. |
| N K | James' and Mary's. |
| N L | James' and Mary's Eastern Gut Track No. 1. |
| N M | James' and Mary's Eastern Gut Track No. 2. |
| N P | James' and Mary's Eastern Gut Track No. 3. |
| N Q | James' and Mary's Eastern Gut Track No. 4. |
| N R | James' and Mary's Eastern Gut Track No. 5. |
| N S | James' and Mary's Western Gut. |
| N V | James' and Mary's Western Gut Track No. 1. |
| N W | James' and Mary's Western Gut Track No. 2. |

# PART IV.

## NAMES OF PLACES, CREEKS, MARKS, &c.

### Rendezvous Flag over Letter.

| LETTRES. | NAMES. |
|---|---|
| P B | James' and Mary's Western Gut Track No. 3. |
| P C | James' and Mary's Western Gut Track No. 4. |
| P D | James' and Mary's Western Gut Track No. 5. |
| P F | James' and Mary's Creek to Creek. |
| P G | James' and Mary's Creek to Creek Track No. 1. |
| P H | James' and Mary's Creek to Creek Track No. 2. |
| P J | James' and Mary's Creek to Creek Track No. 3. |
| P K | Jar Makers. |
| P L | Jar Makers' Reach. |
| P M | Jar Makers' Point. |
| P N | Jellingham Sand. |
| P Q | Jiggercolly. |
| P R | Jiggercolly Semaphore Tower. |
| P S | Kanaka River. |
| P V | Kanaka Bay. |
| P W | Kedgree. |

# PART IV.

## NAMES OF PLACES, CREEKS, MARKS, &c.

### Rendezvous Flag over Letter.

| LETTERS. | NAMES. |
|---|---|
| Q B | Kedgree E. T. Station. |
| Q C | Kedgree Tidal Semaphore. |
| Q D | Kedgree Index Piles. |
| Q F | Kedgree Trees. |
| Q G | Kedgree Point. |
| Q H | Kedgree Roads. |
| Q J | Kedgree Sand. |
| Q K | Kedgree Upper Creek. |
| Q L | Kedgree Lower Creek. |
| Q M | Kell Kiln or S'watch. |
| Q N | Kidderpore. |
| Q P | Kidderpore Dock. |
| Q R | Kookrohatty. |
| Q S | Kookrohatty Lumps. |
| Q V | Kookrohatty Trees. |
| Q W | Kulpee. |

# PART IV.

## NAMES OF PLACES, CREEKS, MARKS, &c.

### Rendezvous Flag over Letter.

| LETTERS. | NAMES. |
|---|---|
| R B | Kulpee Flat. |
| R C | Kulpee Pagoda. |
| R D | Kulpee Grove or Trees. |
| R F | Kulpee Ridge. |
| R G | Kulpee Roads or Anchorage. |
| R H | Kulpee Creek. |
| R J | Kyd's Point. |
| R K | Lacam's Channel. |
| R L | Light House Sand. |
| R M | Light House Sand, Head of. |
| R N | Light House Sand, Tail of. |
| R P | Light House Sand, Eastern edge of. |
| R Q | Light House Sand, Western edge of. |
| R S | Lloyd's Channel. |
| R V | Lloyd's Channel Anchorage. |
| R W | Lloyd's Channel Bar. |

# PART IV.

## NAMES OF PLACES, CREEKS, MARKS, &c.

### Rendezvous Flag over Letter.

| LETTERS. | NAMES. |
|---|---|
| S B | Long Sand. |
| S C | Luff Point. |
| S D | Melancholy Point ⎫ |
| S F | Melancholy Reach ⎬ or Moonecolly. |
| S G | Melancholy Sand ⎭ |
| S H | Middle Ground Eastern Channel. |
| S J | Middle Ground Eastern Channel, Head of. |
| S K | Middle Ground Eastern Channel, Tail of. |
| S L | Middle Ground Eastern Channel, Back of. |
| S M | Middle Ground Eastern Channel, Eastern edge of. |
| S N | Middle Ground Eastern Channel, Western edge of. |
| S P | Middle Ground Western Channel. |
| S Q | Middle Ground Western Channel, Head of. |
| S R | Middle Ground Western Channel, Tail of. |
| S V | Middle Ground Western Channel, Back of. |
| S W | Middle Ground Western Channel, Eastern edge of. |

# PART IV.

## NAMES OF PLACES, CREEKS, MARKS, &c.

### Rendezvous Flag over Letter.

| LETTERS. | NAMES. |
|---|---|
| V B | Middle Ground Western Channel, Western edge of. |
| V C | Middle Point. |
| V D | Middle Point Creek. |
| V F | Middle Point Flat. |
| V G | Mizen Sand. |
| V H | Moyapoor. |
| V J | Moyapoor Upper Crossing Creek. |
| V K | Moyapoor Lower Crossing Creek. |
| V L | Moyapoor Index Piles. |
| V M | Moyapoor Tidal Semaphore. |
| V N | Moyapoor Magazine. |
| V P | Moyapoor Reach. |
| V Q | Moyapoor Flat. |
| V R | Moyapoor Flat Track No. 1. |
| V S | Moyapoor Flat Track No. 2. |
| V W | Moyapoor Flat Track No. 3. |

# PART IV.

## NAMES OF PLACES, CREEKS, MARKS, &c.

### Rendezvous Flag over Letter.

| LETTERS. | NAMES. |
|---|---|
| W B | Moyapoor Flat Track No. 4. |
| W C | Moyapoor Flat Track No. 5. |
| W D | Moyapoor Flat Track No. 6 or Fair Way. |
| W F | Mud Point. |
| W G | Mud Point Channel. |
| W H | Mud Point Channel Anchorage. |
| W J | Mud Point E. T. Station. |
| W K | Mud Point Mark. |
| W L | Mud Point Trees. |
| W M | Mutlah River. |
| W N | Mutlah River Light Station, Outer. |
| W P | Mutlah River Light Station, Inner. |
| W Q | Noorpoor |
| W R | Noorpoor Anchorage |
| W S | Noorpoor Creek |
| W V | Noorpoor Lumps |

Beebee Domingo. *(bracketing Noorpoor entries W Q–W V)*

# PART IV.

## NAMES OF PLACES, CREEKS, MARKS, &c.

### Rendezvous Flag over Letter.

| LETTERS. | NAMES. |
|---|---|
| B C D | Noorpoor Flat |
| B C F | Noorpoor Point |
| B C G | Noorpoor Single Tree }  Beebee Domingo. |
| B C H | Noorpoor Mark, Upper |
| B C J | Noorpoor Mark, Lower |
| B C K | Nynan. |
| B C L | Nynan Creek. |
| B C M | Nynan Lumps. |
| B C N | Nynan Index Piles. |
| B C P | Nynan Ridge or broken ground off Nynan. |
| B C Q | Nynan Double Tree. |
| B C R | Nynan Mark, Upper. |
| B C S | Nynan Mark, Lower. |
| B C V | Peer Serang. |
| B C W | Pilot's Ridge. |

# PART IV.

## NAMES OF PLACES, CREEKS, MARKS, &c.

### Rendezvous Flag over Letter.

| LETTERS. | NAMES. |
|---|---|
| B D C | Pilot's Ridge, Head of. |
| B D F | Pilot's Ridge, Tail of. |
| B D G | Pilot's Ridge, Eastern edge of. |
| B D H | Pilot's Ridge, Western edge of. |
| B D J | Pilot's Ridge Light Station. |
| B D K | Pipley River. |
| B D L | Pipley Sand. |
| B D M | Pitt's Point. |
| B D N | Plowden's Island. |
| B D P | Point Palmyras. |
| B D Q | Point Palmyras Reef. |
| B D R | Point Jelly. |
| B D S | Puppies Parlour. |
| B D V | Raggunge. |
| B D W | Rangafulla. |

# PART IV.

## NAMES OF PLACES, CREEKS, MARKS, &c.

### Rendezvous Flag over Letter.

| Letters. | Names. |
| --- | --- |
| B F C | Rangafulla Channel Outer. |
| B F D | Rangafulla Channel Centre. |
| B F G | Rangafulla Channel Inner. |
| B F H | Rangafulla Channel Outer Bar Upper. |
| B F J | Rangafulla Channel Outer Bar Lower. |
| B F K | Rangafulla Channel Centre Bar Upper. |
| B F L | Rangafulla Channel Centre Bar Lower. |
| B F M | Rangafulla Channel Inner Bar Upper. |
| B F N | Rangafulla Channel Inner Bar Lower. |
| B F P | Rangafulla Tidal Semaphore. |
| B F Q | Rangafulla Index Piles. |
| B F R | Rangafulla Creek. |
| B F S | Rangafulla Ridge. |
| B F V | Rangafulla Ridge Mark. |
| B F W | Rangafulla Island. |

## NAMES OF PLACES, CREEKS, MARKS, &c.

### Rendezvous Flag over Letter.

| LETTERS. | NAMES. |
|---|---|
| B G G | Rangafulla Island Mark. |
| B G D | Rangafulla Obelisk. |
| B G F | Reef Eastern. |
| B G H | Reef Eastern, Head of. |
| B G J | Reef Eastern, Tail of. |
| B G K | Reef Eastern, Eastern Edge of. |
| B G L | Reef Eastern, Western Edge of. |
| B G M | Reef Western. |
| B G N | Reef Western, Head of. |
| B G P | Reef Western, Tail of. |
| B G Q | Reef Western, Eastern Edge of. |
| B G R | Reef Western, Western Edge of. |
| B G S | Reef Head. |
| B G V | Reef Head Breakers. |
| B G W | Reef Head Passage. |

## NAMES OF PLACES, CREEKS, MARKS, &c.

### Rendezvous Flag over Letter.

| LETTERS. | NAMES. |
|---|---|
| B H C | Roopnarain River. |
| B H D | Royapore. |
| B H F | Royapore Reach. |
| B H G | Royapore Sand. |
| B H J | Royapore Index Piles. |
| B H K | Royapore Sister Trees. |
| B H L | Royapore Flat. |
| B H M | Royapore Flat Track No. 1. |
| B H N | Royapore Flat Track No. 2. |
| B H P | Royapore Flat Track No. 3. |
| B H Q | Royapore Flat Track No. 4. |
| B H R | Royapore Flat Track No. 5. |
| B H S | Sangaroll. |
| B H V | Sangaroll Creek. |
| B H W | Sangaroll Reach. |

# PART IV.

## NAMES OF PLACES, CREEKS, MARKS, &c.

### Rendezvous Flag over Letter.

| Letters. | Names. |
|---|---|
| **B J C** | Sangaroll Sand. |
| **B J D** | Sangaroll Village. |
| **B J F** | Saugor. |
| **B J G** | Saugor Bluff. |
| **B J H** | Saugor Flat. |
| **B J K** | Saugor Island. |
| **B J L** | Saugor Light House. |
| **B J M** | Saugor Point. |
| **B J N** | Saugor Point Anchorage. |
| **B J P** | Saugor Roads. |
| **B J Q** | Saugor Creek. |
| **B J R** | Saugor E. T. Station. |
| **B J S** | Saugor Sand. |
| **B J V** | Saugor Sand, Head of. |
| **B J W** | Saugor Sand, Tail of. |

## NAMES OF PLACES, CREEKS, MARKS, &c.

### Rendezvous Flag over Letter.

| LETTERS. | NAMES. |
| --- | --- |
| B K C | Saugor Sand, Eastern Edge of. |
| B K D | Saugor Sand, Western Edge of. |
| B K F | Ship Gunge. |
| B K G | Ship Gunge Creek. |
| B K H | Ship Gunge Mark. |
| B K J | Ship Gunge Point. |
| B K L | Ship Gunge Sand. |
| B K M | Ship Tree Mark North. |
| B K N | Ship Tree Mark Centre. |
| B K P | Ship Tree Mark South. |
| B K Q | Sidney Point. |
| B K R | Silver Tree Obelisk. |
| B K S | Silver Tree Point. |
| B K V | Silver Tree Sand. |
| B K W | Silver Tree Reach. |

## NAMES OF PLACES, CREEKS, MARKS, &c.

### Rendezvous Flag over Letter.

| LETTERS. | NAMES. |
|----------|--------|
| B L C | Swatch of no Ground. |
| B L D | Sumatra Sand. |
| B L F | Sundea Semaphore. |
| B L G | Teetoolbarree Creek (close to Suff Point). |
| B L H | Thornton's Channel. |
| B L J | Thornton's Channel Upper Bar. |
| B L K | Thornton's Channel Lower Bar. |
| B L M | Tuly's Nullah or Creek. |
| B L N | Tumlook. |
| B L P | Tumlook Temple. |
| B L Q | Tumlook Point. |
| B L R | Tumlook Village. |
| B L S | Vauzan's Creek. |
| B L V | Oolabariah. |
| B L W | Oolabariah Creek Upper. |

# PART IV.

## NAMES OF PLACES, CREEKS, MARKS, &c.

### Rendezvous Flag over Letter.

| LETTERS. | NAMES. |
|---|---|
| B M C | Oolabariah Creek Centre. |
| B M D | Oolabariah Creek Lower. |
| B M F | Oolabariah Reach. |
| B M G | Oolabariah Sand. |
| B M J | Oolabariah Village. |
| B M K | Western Channel. |
| B M L | *Muckroputty lumps* |
| B M N | *Port Mornington Flat* |
| B M P | |
| B M Q | |
| B M R | |
| B M S | |
| B M V | |
| B M W | |

# PART V.

## SENTENCES.

No Distinguishing Flag in either Code.

## RIVER SURVEYOR'S SIGNALS.

### Telegraph Flag over Letter.

# PART V.

## SENTENCES.

### No Distinguishing Flag.

PILOT'S CODE. MARRYATT'S CODE.

I HAVE OFFICERS ON BOARD. | I HAVE OFFICERS ON BOARD.

| LEADING WORDS. | LETTERS. | A |
|---|---|---|
| | B | Anchor. |
| | C | Yes. |
| | D | No. |
| | F | Weigh. |
| | G | Come within hail. |
| | H | Tack. |
| | J | Tack and lay to. |
| | K | Wear. |
| | L | Wear and lay to. |
| | M | What Officers have you on board? |
| | N | I have Officers on board. |
| | P | I have no Officers on board. . |
| | Q | Recall *which recalls a Boat.* |
| | R | Wishing to speak the Senior Officer. |
| | S | I wish to speak you. |
| | T | Permission granted. |
| | V | Send for your letters. |
| | W | I have letters for you. |

| LEADING WORDS. | LETTERS. | A |
|---|---|---|
| | B C | Will you take a letter for me ? |
| | B D | A boat with a 2nd Mate or Volunteer. |
| Abandon. | B F | Abandon the Vessel. |
| | B G | Do not abandon the Vessel. |
| Able. | B H | When I am able ? |
| | B J | Are you able. |
| | B K | I am able. |
| | B L | I am not able. |
| | B M | I will be able. |
| | B N | When you are able. |
| Absence. | B P | During my absence. |
| | B Q | During your absence. |
| | B R | In the absence of *Person or Vessel indicated.* |
| Accident. | B S | I have met with an accident. |
| | B T | *Vessel or Person indicated* has met with an accident. |
| Accounts. | B V | Have you had any accounts of *Vessel or Person indicated ?* |
| | B W | I have had no accounts of *Vessel or Person indicated.* |

# PART V.

## SENTENCES.

### No Distinguishing Flag.

| LEADING WORDS. | LETTERS. | A |
|---|---|---|
| Accommo-date. | C B | Can you accommodate a Passenger ? |
| | C D | Can you accommodate a Lady Passenger ? |
| | C F | Can you accommodate an Invalid Passenger ? |
| | C G | I can accommodate an Invalid Passenger. |
| | C H | I can accommodate a Lady Passenger. |
| | C J | I cannot accommodate an Invalid Passenger. |
| | C K | I cannot accommodate a Lady Passenger. |
| Afloat. | C L | Will you be afloat at High Water ? |
| | C M | I will be afloat at High Water. |
| | C N | I will not be afloat at High Water. |
| | C P | Is the *Vessel indicated* afloat ? |
| | C Q | The *Vessel indicated* is afloat. |
| | C R | The *Vessel indicated* is not afloat. |
| | C S | The *Vessel indicated* has floated. |
| | C T | Are you afloat ? |
| | C V | I am afloat. |
| | C W | I am not afloat. |

*I am adrift*
*" have been adrift*
*Ves indicated is adrift*
*"      "   has drifted*
*Signalize to /Ves indicated/ she is adrift!*

# PART V.

## SENTENCES.

### No Distinguishing Flag.

| Leading Words. | Letters. | A |
|---|---|---|
| Agreeable. | D B | I am agreeable. |
| | D C | I am not agreeable. |
| | D F | Are you agreeable ? |
| Aground. | D G | Are you aground ? |
| | D H | Have you been aground ? |
| | D J | *Vessel indicated* is aground. |
| | D K | I am aground. |
| | D L | I am not aground. |
| | D M | I have been  aground. |
| | D N | I am aground, will you anchor near to heave me off ? |
| | D P | I shall be aground at Low Water. |
| | D Q | You will be aground at Low Water *or Vessel indicated*. |
| | D R | I am aground Abaft. |
| | D S | I am aground Amidships. |
| | D T | I am aground Forward. |
| | D V | Report my being aground. |
| | D W | Grounded on her Anchor. |

# PART V.

## SENTENCES.

### No Distinguishing Flag.

| Leading Words. | Letters. | A |
|---|---|---|
| Aground. | F B | Report my having been aground, but floated without damage and proceeded on. |
| | F C | Report my having been aground, but floated with damage and returning. |
| Ahead. | F D | Pass ahead. |
| | F G | Do not pass ahead. |
| Alteration. | F H | Is there any alteration in *Place indicated* ? |
| | F J | There is some alteration. |
| | F K | There is no material alteration. |
| Anchor. | F L | Will you anchor ? |
| | F M | I shall anchor. |
| | F N | Will you anchor during the night ? |
| | F P | I intend to anchor immediately. |
| | F Q | I intend to anchor at High Water. |
| | F R | I intend to anchor at Low Water. |
| | F S | Anchor in company. |
| | F T | I am riding by my last Anchor. |
| | F V | I have lost, *the number of Anchors to follow.* |
| | F W | Anchor well to the Eastward. |

| Leading Words. | Letters. | A |
|---|---|---|
| Anchor. | G B | Anchor well to the Westward. |
| | G C | Anchor well to the Northward. |
| | G D | Anchor well to the Southward. |
| | G F | When I have anchored. |
| | G H | When you have anchored. |
| | G J | When she or *Vessel indicated* has anchored. |
| Anchors & Cables. | G K | I am in want of Anchors and Cables. |
| | G L | Supply me with an Anchor. |
| | G M | I cannot purchase my Anchor, for want of men. |
| | G N | I cannot purchase my Anchor, Crew sick. |
| | G P | I have hooked an Anchor and purchased it, *if any Cable signal to follow.* |
| | G Q | I have hooked an Anchor too heavy to purchase, have slipped with Buoy. |
| | G R | Shall I anchor? |
| | G S | Do not anchor. |
| | G T | I shall not anchor. |
| | G V | Shall I remain at Anchor? |
| | G W | Remain at anchor. |

# PART V.

## SENTENCES.

### No Distinguishing Flag.

| Leading Words. | Letters. | A |
|---|---|---|
| Anchor. | H B | Do not remain at Anchor. |
| | H C | Will you remain at Anchor? |
| | H D | I shall remain at Anchor. |
| | H F | I shall not remain at Anchor. |
| | H G | I shall remain at Anchor till wind changes. |
| | H J | I shall remain at Anchor till weather changes. |
| | H K | I shall remain at Anchor, as I am directed not to leave the Station. |
| | H L | Ridge Light in want of Anchors. |
| | H M | Eastern Channel Light in want of Anchors. |
| | H N | Lower Gasper Light in want of Anchors. |
| | H P | Upper Gasper Light in want of Anchors. |
| | H Q | Shall I anchor during the night? |
| | H R | Anchor during the night. |
| | H S | Do not anchor during the night. |
| | H T | I shall anchor during the night. |
| | H V | I shall not anchor during the night. |
| | H W | Shall I remain at Anchor during the night? |

## SENTENCES.

### No Distinguishing Flag.

| LEADING WORDS. | LETTERS. | A |
|---|---|---|
| Anchor. | J B | Remain at Anchor during the night. |
| | J C | Do not remain at Anchor during the night. |
| | J D | Will you remain at Anchor during the night? |
| | J F | I shall remain at Anchor during the night. |
| | J G | I shall not remain at Anchor during the night. |
| | J H | When do you intend to anchor ? |
| | J K | Where do you intend to anchor ? |
| | J L | I intend to anchor at *Time or Place indicated.* |
| | J M | I cannot anchor without danger. |
| | J N | Anchor North and South of each other. |
| | J P | Anchor East and West of each other. |
| | J Q | Anchor well to *Quarter indicated.* |
| | J R | Anchor on *Place indicated.* |
| | J S | Anchor near me in *Place indicated.* |
| | J T | Trip your Anchor. |
| | J V | Will you lead me into Anchorage. |
| | J W | I will lead you into Anchorage. |

# PART V.

## SENTENCES.

### No Distinguishing Flag.

| LEADING WORDS. | LETTERS. | A |
|---|---|---|
| Anchor. | K B | You will find Anchorage at *Place or Buoy indicated.* |
| | K C | You will not find Anchorage at *Place or Buoy indicated.* |
| | K D | There is Anchorage of *No. of feet indicated* at Low Water. |
| | K F | I have but one Anchor left. |
| | K G | I have no Anchor left. |
| | K H | I am in want of Anchors. |
| | K J | She or *Vessel indicated* has lost an Anchor or *No. indicated.* |
| | K L | She or *Vessel indicated* has but one Anchor left or *No. indicated.* |
| | K M | She or *Vessel indicated* has no Anchor left. |
| | K N | She or *Vessel indicated* is in want of Anchors. |
| | K P | Will you supply me or her with an Anchor? |
| | K Q | I will supply you or *Vessel indicated* with an Anchor. |
| | K R | I will supply you or *Vessel indicated* with an Anchor, *Time and Place indicated.* |
| | K S | Supply *Vessel indicated* with an Anchor. |
| | K T | I have no Anchor to spare. |
| | K V | How many Anchors have you on board ? |
| | K W | I am obliged to slip from my Anchor. |

# PART V.

## SENTENCES.

### No Distinguishing Flag.

| Leading Words. | Letters. | A |
|---|---|---|
| Anchor. | L B | I have been obliged to slip from my Anchor to avoid collision. |
| | L C | I have been obliged to slip from my Anhor to avoid grounding. |
| | L D | Slip from your Anchor and go to Sea. |
| | L F | Slip from your Anchor and run in. |
| | L G | Buoy and slip your Anchor. |
| | L H | My Anchor is buried. |
| | L J | Your Anchor is foul. |
| | L K | Are you in want of an Anchor or Anchor. |
| | L M | I have recovered your Anchor. |
| | L N | I have lost Anchors *No. indicated.* |
| Annulled. | L P | Signals made are annulled. |
| | L Q | The particular Signal following is annulled. |
| Answer. | L R | Send me an answer as soon as possible. |
| | L S | Send me an answer when convenient. |
| | L T | What is the answer? |
| | L V | Remain for the answer. |
| | L W | I shall remain for the answer. |

# PART V.

## SENTENCES.

### No Distinguishing Flag.

| Leading Words. | Letters. | A |
|---|---|---|
| April. | M B | April. |
| Arrange. | M C | Will you leave it to my arrangement? |
| | M D | I will leave it to your arrangement. |
| | M F | Do not arrange before communicating with me. |
| | M G | Arrange as most beneficial to public service. |
| | M H | Shall I arrange? |
| Arrest. | M J | I have placed under arrest *Officer's name to follow.* |
| | M K | Shall I send Officer under arrest on board? |
| | M L | Shall I send Officer under arrest to Calcutta? |
| | M N | Send Officer on board with a full report of case. |
| | M P | Keep Officer on board, and send me a full report of case. |
| | M Q | Send Officer under arrest to Calcutta, with full report of case. |
| | M R | Keep Officer under arrest till further orders. |
| Arrive. | M S | When do you expect *Person or Vessel indicated* to arrive? |
| | M T | *Person or Vessel indicated* is expected on *date indicated.* |
| | M V | *Person or Vessel indicated* has arrived. |
| | M W | *Person or Vessel indicated* has not arrived. |

# PART V.

## SENTENCES.

### No Distinguishing Flag.

| Leading Words. | Letters | A |
|---|---|---|
| Assistance. | N B | I require assistance. |
| | N C | Do you require assistance ? |
| | N D | I do not require assistance. |
| | N F | Will you assist me into safety ? |
| | N G | Will you assist me or *Vessel indicated* ? |
| | N H | Can you assist me or *Vessel indicated* ? |
| | N J | *Vessel indicated* is in want of assistance. |
| | N K | Will you assist in transporting Stores ? |
| | N L | Will you assist in taking Pilots from Ships ? |
| | N M | Will you assist in supplying Pilots to Ships ? |
| | N P | I will give every assistance to *Vessel indicated*. |
| | N Q | I cannot assist you or *Vessel indicated*. |
| | N R | I will give every assistance when weather moderates. |
| | N S | I will give every assistance at *Time or Place indicated*. |
| | N T | I shall remain for assistance. |
| | N V | What assistance is required. ? |
| | N W | The assistance required is *as indicated*. |

# PART V.

## SENTENCES.

### No Distinguishing Flag.

| Leading Words. | Letters. | A |
|---|---|---|
| **Assistance.** | P B | Go to the assistance of *Vessel indicated.* |
| | P C | Report by Telegram, I am in want of immediate assistance. |
| | P D | Endeavour to obtain assistance for me or *Vessel indicated.* |
| | P F | I will endeavour to obtain assistance for you or *Vessel indicated.* |
| **Astern.** | P G | Pass astern. |
| | P H | Do not pass astern. |
| | P J | I shall pass astern. |
| | P K | Do not keep so far astern. |
| **Attempt.** | P L | Attempt it. |
| | P M | Do not attempt it. |
| | P N | Shall I attempt it? |
| | P Q | Will you attempt it? |
| | P R | I shall not attempt it till weather moderates. |
| | P S | I shall not attempt it till wind changes. |
| | P T | I shall not attempt it till springs lift. |
| | P V | I shall not attempt it. |
| | P W | I shall attempt it. |

# PART V.

## SENTENCES.

### No Distinguishing Flag.

| Leading Words. | Letters. | A |
|---|---|---|
| Attend-ance. | Q B | I am in want of Medical attendance. |
| | Q C | *Vessel indicated* is in want of Medical attendance. |
| | Q D | Attend Vessel in distress into safety. |
| | Q F | Attend Vessel in distress till further orders. |
| | Q G | Attend Vessel in distress till no longer required. |
| August. | Q H | August. |
| Authority. | Q J | By whose authority. |
| | Q K | By authority of *Person indicated.* |
| | Q L | |
| | Q M | |
| | Q N | |
| | Q P | |
| * | Q R | I hold an application, can I return?* |
| | Q S | |
| | Q T | |
| | Q V | |
| | Q W | |

\* If the Officer carries a Private Flag, it is to be shown *below the Signal,* if not his Number in Part I.

# PART V.

## SENTENCES.

### No Distinguishing Flag.

| Leading Words. | Letters. | B |
|---|---|---|
| Bar. | R B | What water will there be on the Bar to-day ? |
| | R C | What water will there be on the Upper Bar to-day ? |
| | R D | What water will there be on the Centre Bar to-day ? |
| | R F | What water will there be on the Lower Bar to-day ? |
| | R G | There will be *No. of feet indicated* on Bar to-day at low water. |
| | R H | There will be *No. of feet indicated* on Upper Bar to-day at low water. |
| | R J | There will be *No. of feet indicated* on Centre Bar to-day at low water. |
| | R K | There will be *No. of feet indicated* on Lower Bar to-day at low water. |
| | R L | Shall I find water to cross the Bar to-day ? *Vessel's draft to follow.* |
| | R M | I think the tide will rise sufficiently, to enable you to cross the Bar to-day. |
| | R N | I do not think the tide will rise sufficiently to enable you to cross the Bar to-day. |
| | R P | Will you signalize in what water you cross the Bar? |
| | R Q | What water on the Bar ? |
| | R S | Do not attempt to cross the Bar. |
| | R T | Water on the Bar has shallowed. |
| | R V | Water on the Bar has deepened. |
| | R W | Bar has changed its direction to the North. |

# PART V.

## SENTENCES.

### No Distinguishing Flag.

| LEADING WORDS. | LETTERS. | B |
|---|---|---|
| Bar. | S B | Bar has changed its direction to the South. |
| | S C | Bar has changed its direction to the East. |
| | S D | Bar has changed its direction to the West. |
| | S F | Vessel wrecked on the Bar, *bearings to follow.* |
| | S G | Will you lead across the Bar ? |
| | S H | I will lead across the Bar. |
| | S J | Follow me across the Bar. |
| Barometer. | S K | What is the height of your Barometer ? |
| | S L | Barometer is rising. |
| | S M | Barometer is falling. |
| | S N | Barometer is stationary. |
| | S P | What weather does your Barometer indicate ? |
| | S Q | Barometer indicates moderate weather. |
| | S R | Barometer indicates a gale. |
| | S T | Barometer indicates fine weather. |
| | S V | Is your Barometer rising or falling ? |
| | S W | I have no Barometer. |

# PART V.

## SENTENCES.

### No Distinguishing Flag.

| Leading Words. | Letters. | B |
|---|---|---|
| Barometer. | B C D | My Barometer is injured. |
| Bear—up. | B C F | How does my Vessel bear from you ? *answered by Compass Signal Part VI.* |
| | B C G | Bear up immediately. |
| | B C H | I shall bear up immediately. |
| | B C J | I will send you instructions when to bear up. |
| | B C K | She or *Vessel indicated* has borne up. |
| | B C L | When will you bear up ? |
| | B C M | I shall bear up at *time indicated*. |
| Bearing. | B C N | How does *Vessel, Buoy, place or mark indicated* bear of you ? |
| | B C P | Vessel, Buoy, place or mark bear of me *as indicated*. |
| | B C Q | How did *Vessel, Buoy, place or mark indicated* bear of you when last seen ? |
| | B C R | Vessel, Buoy, place or mark bore of me when last seen *as indicated*. |
| Berth. | B C S | Will you lead me into a good berth ? |
| | B C T | I will lead you into a good berth. |
| | B C V | Lead *Vessel indicate*ood into a gd berth. |
| | B C W | Take up the berth *as indicated*. |

## SENTENCES.

### No Distinguishing Flag.

| LEADING WORDS. | LETTERS. | B |
|---|---|---|
| **Blow.** | B D C | It blows too hard. |
| | B D F | Should it blow hard from *quarter indicated*? |
| **Blown off.** | B D G | I have been blown off the Station. |
| | B D H | *Vessel indicated* has been blown off. |
| **Blue Light Composition.** | B D J | There is no blue light composition on the Station. |
| | B D K | Proceed to Eastern Channel for blue light composition. |
| | B D L | Proceed to Gasper Channel for blue light composition. |
| | B D M | Proceed to Ridge Light for blue light composition. |
| | B D N | I sighted a blue light last night, *hour and bearing as indicated*. |
| | B D P | Show a blue light every *No. of hours indicated*. |
| | B D Q | I shall show a blue light every *No. of hours as indicated*. |
| | B D R | I am in want of blue light composition. |
| | B D S | I have blue light composition for *days indicated*. |
| | B D T | Are you in want of blue light composition? |
| | B D V | I am not in want of blue light composition? |
| | B D W | Supply *Vessel indicated* with blue light composition. |

# PART V.

## SENTENCES.

### No Distinguishing Flag.

| LEADING WORDS. | LETTERS. | B |
|---|---|---|
| Blue Light. | B F C | I have empty blue light barrels on board. |
| | B F D | Will you take empty blue light barrels to Town ? |
| | B F G | I have been burning extra blue lights. |
| | B F H | *Vessel indicated* is in want of blue light composition. |
| | B F J | I have blue light composition for you or *Vessel indicated.* |
| | B F K | Show a blue light if you sight *Vessel indicated,* or strike soundings on *place indicated.* |
| | B F L | I will show a blue light on sighting *Vessel indicated,* or strike soundings on *place indicated.* |
| Board. | B F M | Branch Pilot to come on board in his boat. |
| | B F N | Will you come on board ? |
| | B F P | I will go on board. |
| | B F Q | I cannot go on board. |
| | B F R | Who have you on board ? |
| | B F S | I have on board *as indicated.* |
| | B F T | Have you on board *as indicated* ? |
| | B F V | Come on board. |
| | B F W | Shall I go on board ? |

## SENTENCES.

### No Distinguishing Flag.

| Leading Words. | Letters. | B |
|---|---|---|
| Board. | B G C | Allow *person indicated* to come on board. |
| | B G D | Send on board *as indicated*. |
| | B G F | I have been run on board of by a vessel and sustained damage. |
| | B G H | I have been run on board of by a vessel and sustained no damage. |
| Boat. | B G J | I shall not send my boat. |
| | B G K | Send letter or message by boat. |
| | B G L | Make sail ahead and drop a boat alongside. |
| | B G M | Steam ahead and drop a boat alongside. |
| | B G N | I have lost my starboard quarter boat. |
| | B G P | I have lost my port quarter boat. |
| | B G Q | I have lost all my boats. |
| | B G R | Pick up my boat. |
| | B G S | Pick up the boat adrift. |
| | B G T | The boat is lost but crew are saved. |
| | B G V | The boat is lost and part of the crew saved. |
| | B G W | The boat is lost and none of the crew saved. |

| Leading Words. | Letters. | B |
|---|---|---|
| Boat. | B H C | A boat with a Branch Pilot. |
| | B H D | A boat with a Master Pilot. |
| | B H F | A boat with a Mate. |
| | B H G | A boat with a 2nd Mate. |
| | B H J | My large boat is useless, will you change? |
| | B H K | My small boat is useless, will you change? |
| | B H L | Will you take my large boat to Town? |
| | B H M | Will you take my small boat to Town? |
| | B H N | My boat is adrift. |
| | B H P | My boat cannot stem the tide. |
| | B H Q | A ship has run over my boat, crew saved. |
| | B H R | A ship has run over my boat, crew missing. |
| | B H S | Shall I send my boat? |
| | B H T | Send your boat. |
| | B H V | Do not send your boat. |
| | B H W | Will you send your boat? |

# PART V..

## SENTENCES.

### No Distinguishing Flag.

| Leading Words. | Letters. | B |
|---|---|---|
| Boat. | B J C | I will send my boat. |
| | B J D | Send a boat on board *Vessel indicated*. |
| | B J F | I will send a boat on board *Vessel indicated*. |
| | B J G | Do not detain my boat. |
| | B J H | There is too much sea for my boat. |
| | B J K | The vessel rolls so heavily, it is not safe to lower my boat. |
| | B J L | My boat is leaky or not in a fit state to be sent away. |
| | B J M | My boat is away. |
| | B J N | I will make sail ahead and drop a boat alongside. |
| | B J P | I will make steam ahead and drop a boat alongside. |
| | B J Q | Send a line by boat to facilitate communication. |
| | B J R | Have you saved the boat ? |
| | B J S | The boat is saved. |
| | B J T | The boat is lost. |
| | B J V | Boat capsized, all boats to be sent from vessels near to save crew. |
| | B J W | All boats to be sent to the assistance of vessels in distress. |

# PART V.

## SENTENCES.

### No Distinguishing Flag.

| L EADING WORDS. | LETTERS. | B |
|---|---|---|
| Boat. | B K C | All boats to be sent to tow vessel out of danger. |
| | B K D | Will you send your boat to sound in *direction indicated?* |
| | B K F | I will send my boat to sound for your guidance. |
| | B K G | Saugor Electric Telegraph Boat. |
| | B K H | Mud Point Electric Telegraph Boat. |
| | B K J | Diamond Harbour Electric Telegraph Boat. |
| | B K L | Diamond Harbour Dâk Boat. |
| | B K M | Diamond Harbour Custom House Boat. |
| | B K N | Diamond Harbour Row Boat. |
| | B K P | Hooghly Point Electric Telegraph Boat. |
| | B K Q | Hooghly Point Row Boat. |
| | B K R | Hooghly Point Sounding Boat. |
| | B K S | Moyapore Sounding Boat. |
| | B K T | Moyapore Electric Telegraph Boat. |
| | B K V | My boat is damaged and under repair. |
| | B K W | I require a Dâk Boat. |

| Leading Words. | Letters. | B |
|---|---|---|
| **Boat.** | B L C | I am in want of Tow Boats. |
| | B L D | I do not want a Tow Boat. |
| | B L F | Will you send your Tow Boat to me or to *place indicated?* |
| | B L G | I will send my Tow Boat to you. |
| | B L H | I am going to send my Tow Boat to *place indicated* for or with letters. |
| | B L J | Will you lay your Tow Boat in the best water for crossing? |
| | B L K | My Tow Boat is lying in the best water for crossing. |
| | B L M | I am going in my Tow Boat to sound now or at *time indicated.* |
| **Bowsprit.** | B L N | I have sprung my bowsprit. |
| | B L P | *Vessel indicated* has sprung her bowsprit. |
| | B L Q | My or *vessel indicated* bowsprit is rotten. |
| **Buoy's position.** | B L R | *Buoy indicated* is not laid in proper position. |
| | B L S | *Buoy indicated* is too far North. |
| | B L T | *Buoy indicated* is too far South. |
| | B L V | *Buoy indicated* is too far East. |
| | B L W | *Buoy indicated* is too far West. |

*Boat adrift lay as indicated*
*Signalize to the indicated boat*
*adrift Warning as indicated*
*My boat is adrift*

*You. ( 88„ )*  „   ··
*, Ves indicated, boat is adrift*

| LEADING WORDS. | LETTERS. | B |
|---|---|---|
| Buoys' Places. | B M C | Are all the Buoys in their places ? |
| | B M D | All the Buoys are in their places. |
| | B M F | All the Buoys are not in their places. |
| Buoy adrift, fouled and sunk. | B M G | *Buoy indicated* is adrift. |
| | B M H | *Buoy indicated* has sunk. |
| | B M J | *Buoy indicated* has been fouled and sunk. |
| | B M K | *Buoy indicated* has been fouled, basket and spire gone. |
| Buoy relaid. | B M L | Is Buoy indicated relaid ? |
| | B M N | *Buoy indicated* is relaid. |
| | B M P | *Buoy indicated* is not relaid. |
| | B M Q | Are you going to relay *Buoy indicated ?* |
| | B M R | I am going to relay *Buoy indicated.* |
| | B M S | I am not going to relay *Buoy indicated.* |
| Buoying off Channels. | B M T | Your services are required to buoy off Channel *as indicated.* |
| | B M V | I will send necessary instructions for buoying off Channel *as indicated.* |
| | B M W | Send me full instructions for buoying off Channel *as indicated.* |

# PART V.

## SENTENCES.

### No Distinguishing Flag.

| Leading Words. | Letters. | B |
|---|---|---|
| | B N C | *Buoy indicated* has drifted to *quarter indicated.* |
| Buoys shifted. | B N D | Has *Buoy indicated* been shifted? |
| | B N F | *Buoy indicated* has been shifted. |
| | B N G | *Buoy indicated* has not been shifted. |
| | B N H | Are you going to shift *Buoy indicated?* |
| | B N J | I am going to shift *Buoy indicated.* |
| | B N K | I am not going to shift *Buoy indicated.* |
| Buoys taken away. | B N L | Is *Buoy indicated* taken away? |
| | B N M | *Buoy indicated* is taken away. |
| | B N P | *Buoy indicated* is not taken away. |
| | B N Q | Are you going to take away *Buoy indicated?* |
| | B N R | I am going to take away *Buoy indicated.* |
| | B N S | I am not going to take away *Buoy indicated.* |
| | B N T | Has a Buoy been laid on *place indicated?* |
| | B N V | A Buoy has been laid on *place indicated.* |
| | B N W | A Buoy has not been laid on *place indicated.* |

## SENTENCES.

### No Distinguishing Flag.

| Leading Words. | Letters. | B |
|---|---|---|
| Buoys. | B P C | Has a Buoy been laid on the wreck at *place indicated?* |
| | B P D | A Buoy has been laid on the wreck at *place indicated.* |
| | B P F | A Buoy has not been laid on the wreck at *place indicated.* |
| | B P G | A red Buoy. |
| | B P H | A black Buoy. |
| | B P J | A white Buoy. |
| | B P K | A white and black-painted vertical Buoy. |
| | B P L | A white and black-painted horizontal Buoy. |
| | B P M | A green Buoy. |
| | B P N | An iron Buoy. |
| | B P Q | A nun Buoy. |
| | B P R | A spire Buoy. |
| | B P S | A wreck Buoy. |
| | B P T | The Buoys are now properly *placed* in *Channel indicated.* |
| | B P V | Assist the Buoy vessel in laying *Buoy indicated.* |
| | B P W | Will you assist by anchoring, or lying too, close to *Buoy indicated?* |

# PART V.

## SENTENCES.

### No Distinguishing Flag.

| LEADING WORDS. | LETTERS. | B |
|---|---|---|
| Buoys. | B Q C | Have you seen any of the Buoys ? |
| | B Q D | On sighting a Buoy will you hoist your Ensign ? |
| | B Q F | Have you seen *Buoy indicated?* |
| | B Q G | Look out for *Buoy indicated.* |
| | B Q H | I have not seen *Buoy indicated.* |
| | B Q J | What Buoy is that bearing *as indicated?* |
| | B Q K | The Buoy in sight is *as indicated.* |
| | B Q L | A Buoy adrift bearing *as indicated.* |
| | B Q M | What Buoy is that adrift bearing *as indicated?* |
| | B Q N | The Buoy adrift *is as indicated.* |
| | B Q P | A Buoy ashore at *place indicated.* |
| | B Q R | Pass a Buoy astern. |
| Buoy Station Brig. | B Q S | How does the Buoy Station Brig bear ? |
| | B Q T | How was the Buoy Station Brig bearing when last seen ? |
| | B Q V | At what time was the Buoy Station Brig last seen ? |
| | B Q W | Buoy Station Brig has gone to sea. |

# PART V.

## SENTENCES.

### No Distinguishing Flag.

| LEADING WORDS. | LETTERS. | B |
|---|---|---|
| Buoy Station Brig. | B R C | Buoy Station Brig has gone in. |
| | B R D | Buoy Station Brig is to windward. |
| | B R F | Buoy Station Brig is to leeward. |
| | B R G | Buoy Station Brig bears *as indicated*. |
| | B R H | Is on board. |
| | B R J | |
| | B R K | |

| Leading Words. | Letters. | C |
|---|---|---|
| Cable. | B R L | Ridge Light in want of Cables. |
| | B R M | Eastern Channel Light in want of Cables. |
| | B R N | Lower Gasper Light in want of Cables. |
| | B R P | Upper Gasper Light in want of Cables. |
| | B R Q | I am riding by my last Cable. |
| | B R S | I have parted from my last Cable. |
| | B R T | *Vessel indicated* is riding by her last Cable. |
| | B R V | *Vessel indicated* has parted from her last Cable. |
| | B R W | I am in want of Cables. |

# PART V.

## SENTENCES.

### No Distinguishing Flag.

| LEADING WORDS. | LETTERS. | C |
|---|---|---|
| Cable. | B S C | *Vessel indicated* is in want of Cables. |
| | B S D | Will you supply me ro *Vessel indicated* with a Cable? |
| | B S F | I will supply you or *Vessel indicated* with a Cable. |
| | B S G | Supply me with a Cable. |
| | B S H | Supply *Vessel indicated* with a Cable. |
| | B S J | I cannot supply you or *Vessel indicated* with a Cable. |
| | B S K | How many fathoms of Cable have you on board? |
| | B S L | I have on board of Cable *fathoms indicated*. |
| | B S M | Report I am in want of Cables. |
| | B S N | Report *Vessel indicated* in want of Cables. |
| | B S P | I slipt from Cable last night to prevent collision. |
| | B S Q | Are you in want of Cables? |
| | B S R | Slip from your Cable. |
| | B S T | I have hooked a Cable. |
| | B S V | I have parted from Cable *fathoms indicated*. |
| Capsized. | B S W | Vessel capsized at *place indicated*; crew saved. |

# PART V.

## SENTENCES.

### No Distinguishing Flag.

| Leading Words. | Letters. | C |
|---|---|---|
| Capsized. | B T C | Vessel capsized at *place indicated*; crew lost. |
| | B T D | Are you in danger of capsizing ? |
| Capstan. | B T F | My Capstan is injured. |
| Carried off. | B T G | Officer as *indicated* has been carried off in Ship. |
| | B T H | Officer as *indicated* has been carried off in English Mail Steamer. |
| | B T J | Officer as *indicated* has been carried off in French Mail Steamer. |
| | B T K | Officer as *indicated* has been carried off in China Mail Steamer. |
| | B T L | Officer as *indicated* has been carried off in West Coast Mail Steamer. |
| | B T M | Officer as *indicated* has been carried off in East Coast Mail Steamer. |
| Cartridges. | B T N | I am in want of Cartridges. |
| | B T P | Can you supply me with Cartridges ? |
| | B T Q | I can supply you with Cartridges. |
| | B T R | I cannot supply you with Cartridges. |
| Channel. | B T S | I will lead through *Channel indicated* and show the water. |
| | B T V | I am not acquainted with *Channel indicated*. |
| | B T W | Channel *as indicated* is deeper. |

| Leading Words. | Letters. | C |
|---|---|---|
| **Channel.** | B V C | Channel *as indicated* is shoaler. |
| | B V D | Channel *as indicated* is closed. |
| | B V F | Channel *as indicated* is open. |
| | B V G | Which Channel will you take ? |
| | B V H | Working up Channel. |
| | B V J | Working down Channel. |
| | B V K | Running up Channel. |
| | B V L | Running down Channel. |
| **Channel, Eastern.** | B V M | Are you going to Eastern Channel ? |
| | B V N | I am going to Eastern Channel. |
| | B V P | I am not going to Eastern Channel. |
| | B V Q | Proceed to Eastern Channel. |
| | B V R | What Vessels are there in Eastern Channel ? |
| | B V S | *Vessels indicated* are in Eastern Channel. |
| | B V T | No Vessels in Eastern Channel. |
| | B V W | How many Vessels want Pilots in Eastern Channel ? |

# PART V.

## SENTENCES.

### No Distinguishing Flag.

| LEADING WORDS. | LETTERS. | C |
|---|---|---|
| Channel, Eastern. | B W C | There are *No. indicated* wanting Pilots in Eastern Channel. |
| | B W D | Keep on the Eastern side of Channel. |
| Channel, Western. | B W F | Are you going to Western Channel ? |
| | B W G | I am going to Western Channel. |
| | B W H | I am not going to Western Channel. |
| | B W J | Proceed to Western Channel. |
| | B W K | What Vessels are there in Western Channel ? |
| | B W L | *Vessels indicated* are in Western Channel. |
| | B W M | No Vessels in Western Channel. |
| | B W N | How many Vessels want Pilots in Western Channel ? |
| | B W P | There are *No. indicated* want Pilots in Western Channel. |
| Chart. | B W Q | Can you furnish me with last Chart of *Channel indicated?* |
| | B W R | I can furnish you with last Chart of *Channel indicated.* |
| | B W S | I cannot furnish you with Chart of *Channel indicated.* |
| | B W T | Keep on the Western side of the *Channel indicated.* |
| | B W V | Is there any change in *Channel indicated* since last report ? |

# PART V.

## SENTENCES.

### No Distinguishing Flag.

| Leading Words. | Letters. | C |
|---|---|---|
| Circum-stances. | C B D | Under what circumstances ? |
| | C B F | Under present circumstances. |
| Close. | C B G | Keep close to me. |
| | C B H | Keep close to me during the night. |
| | C B J | I will keep close to you. |
| | C B K | I will keep close to you during the night. |
| | C B L | Do not keep too close to me. |
| | C B M | Do not keep too close to me during the night. |
| | C B N | Keep close enough for me to see your lights during the night. |
| Collision. | C B P | A Vessel has been in collision ; no damage done. |
| | C B Q | A Vessel has been in collision ; slight damage done. |
| | C B R | A Vessel has been in collision ; serious damage done. |
| Command-er. | C B S | Have you my Commander on Board ? |
| | C B T | I have your Commander on Board. |
| | C B V | Commander is sick, and requires medical assistance. |
| | C B W | Commander is sick, and requires to be relieved. |

# PART V.

## SENTENCES.

### No Distinguishing Flag.

| Leading Words. | Letters. | C |
|---|---|---|
| **Commander.** | C D B | Place the Senior Officer in Command. |
| | C D F | Is there any one on Board you can place in Command ? |
| | C D G | Select a fit Officer for Command. |
| | C D H | Commander of *Vessel indicated* granted leave requires to be relieved. |
| | C D J | Commander of *Vessel indicated* ordered to town requires to be relieved. |
| **Communication.** | C D K | I wish to communicate. |
| | C D L | Will you communicate as soon as possible ? |
| | C D M | I will communicate as soon as possible. |
| | C D N | I will communicate at High Water. |
| | C D P | I will communicate at Low Water. |
| | C D Q | I will communicate when Pilots are taken out of Vessels near. |
| | C D R | I will communicate when Pilots are supplied to Vessels near. |
| | C D S | I will communicate when under weigh. |
| | C D T | I will communicate at *time indicated*. |
| | C D V | I will communicate when wind changes. |
| | C D W | I will communicate when finished cleaning below. |

# PART V.

## SENTENCES.

### No Distinguishing Flag.

| LEADING WORDS. | LETTERS. | C |
|---|---|---|
| **Communi-cation.** | C F B | I will communicate with you now. |
| | C F D | Too much sea to communicate by boat. |
| | C F G | Have you communicated with *Vessel or place indicated?* |
| | C F H | I have communicated with *Vessel or place indicated.* |
| | C F J | I have not communicated with *Vessel or place indicated.* |
| | C F K | I have received the following communication. |
| | C F L | Communicate for the information of *person indicated.* |
| | C F M | Communicate your wants by Electric Telegraph. |
| **Company.** | C F N | I will keep company with you. |
| | C F P | I will keep company with you till you are in safety or to *indicated place.* |
| | C F Q | Keep company with me. |
| | C F R | Shall I keep company with you? |
| | C F S | Will you keep company till I am in safety or at *place indicated?* |
| | C F T | Keep company with *Vessel indicated* until in safety or to *place indicated.* |
| | C F V | I will keep company and take you out in smoother water. |
| | C F W | I will keep company and take the Officers out in smoother water. |

# PART V.

## SENTENCES.

### No Distinguishing Flag.

| Leading Words. | Letters. | C |
|---|---|---|
| Company. | C G B | I will keep company till we are at Ridge Light Station. |
| | C G D | I will keep company till we are at Eastern Channel Light Station. |
| | C G F | I will keep company till we are at Saugor. |
| | C G H | Thanks for keeping company. |
| | C G J | Circumstances prevent my keeping company. |
| | C G K | No occasion to keep company. |
| Convenient. | C G L | When will it be convenient? |
| | C G M | It will be convenient now or at *time indicated*. |
| | C G N | It is not convenient. |
| Course. | C G P | Continue your present course. |
| | C G Q | Go on course *indicated*. |
| | C G R | Follow my course. |
| Crew. | C G S | How are the sick Crew left on Board for medical advice? |
| | C G T | Are the sick Crew left on Board now fit for duty? |
| | C G V | Are the sick Crew left on Board better? |
| | C G W | Are the sick Crew left on Board worse? |

# PART V.

## SENTENCES.

### No Distinguishing Flag.

| Leading Words. | Letters. | C |
|---|---|---|
| Crew. | C H B | The sick Crew are fit for duty. |
| | C H D | The sick Crew are better. |
| | C H F | The sick Crew are worse. |
| | C H G | The sick Crew are dead. |
| | C H J | The sick Crew are gone to Calcutta. |
| | C H K | I will send your sick Crew on Board now or at *time indicated.* |
| | C H L | I will send your sick Crew when able. |
| | C H M | Send for the Crew left on Board sick. |
| | C H N | I have part of your Crew on Board. |
| | C H P | Have you my Crew on Board ? |
| | C H Q | I have your Crew on Board. |
| | C H R | I have not your Crew on Board. |
| | C H S | I have on Board some of the Crew of *Vessel indicated.* |
| | C H T | My Crew are sick. |
| | C H V | My Crew are fatigued. |
| | C H W | I have your relief Crew on Board. |

## SENTENCES.

### No Distinguishing Flag.

| Leading Words. | Letters. | C |
|---|---|---|
| Crew. | C J B | I will take your relief Crew to Town. |
| | C J D | I will take your sick Crew to Town. |
| | C J F | Will you take my relief Crew to Town ? |
| | C J G | My Crew are too fatigued; you must come in Ship's boat. |
| Cruizing Brig. | C J H | How does Cruizing Brig bear ? |
| | C J K | How was Cruizing Brig bearing when last seen ? |
| | C J L | At what time was Cruizing Brig last seen ? |
| | C J M | Cruizing Brig has gone to sea. |
| | C J N | Cruizing Brig has gone in. |
| | C J P | |
| | C J Q | |
| | C J R | |

# PART V.

## SENTENCES.

### No Distinguishing Flag.

| LEADING WORDS. | LETTERS. | D |
|---|---|---|
| Damage. | C J S | Have you sustained any damage ? |
| | C J T | I have sustained no damage. |
| | C J V | I have sustained slight damage. |
| | C J W | I have sustained serious damage. |

# PART V.

## SENTENCES.

### No Distinguishing Flag.

| Leading Words. | Letters. | D |
|---|---|---|
| Damage. | C K B | Can you repair damage without assistance ? |
|  | C K D | I can repair damage without assistance. |
|  | C K F | I cannot repair damage without assistance. |
|  | C K G | I must proceed to Saugor to repair damage. |
|  | C K H | I must proceed to Diamond Harbour to repair damage. |
|  | C K J | I must proceed to Calcutta to repair damage. |
|  | C K L | State if possible damages sustained by signal. |
|  | C K M | State damages sustained in a report. |
|  | C K N | How long will it take to repair damage ? |
|  | C K P | To repair damage will take *time indicated.* |
| Danger. | C K Q | You are running into danger. |
|  | C K R | *Vessel indicated* is running into danger. |
|  | G K S | There is danger in your proceeding under present circumstances. |
|  | C K T | Stand from and towards danger for my guidance. |
|  | C K V | Lead the Vessel in sight out of danger. |
| Date. | C K W | Date *as indicated.* |

## SENTENCES.

### No Distinguishing Flag.

| Leading Words. | Letters. | D |
|---|---|---|
| Date. | G L B | From the date of his arrival at Sand-heads. |
| | C L D | From the date of his order. |
| | C L F | From the date of his order reaching Sandheads. |
| | C L G | From this date. |
| Day. | C L H | What day ? |
| | G L J | Days. |
| | C L K | A day. |
| | C L M | To-day. |
| | C L N | Yesterday. |
| | G L P | Day before yesterday. |
| December. | C L Q | December. |
| Departure. | C L R | Has anything occurred since my depar-ture ? |
| | C L S | Have any Vessels past out ? |
| | G L T | Have any Vessels past in ? |
| Detain. | C L V | Do not detain me longer than requisite. |
| | C L W | I must detain you till *time indicated* has elapsed. |

# PART V.

—

## SENTENCES.

### No Distinguishing Flag.

| Leading Words. | Letters. | D |
|---|---|---|
| Detain. | C M B | Is she or *Vessel indicated* detained ? |
| | C M D | She or *Vessel indicated* is detained. |
| | C M F | She or *Vessel indicated* is not detained. |
| | C M G | *Vessel indicated* is detained at *place indicated.* |
| | C M H | What are you detained for ? |
| | C M J | I am detained *as indicated.* |
| Detention. | C M K | Report my detention by Electric Telegraph. |
| | C M L | Report my detention by letter. |
| Dining. | C M N | I will dine with you. |
| | C M P | Will you dine with me ? |
| | C M Q | I shall not be able to dine with you. |
| | C M R | *Person indicated* is dining with me. |
| Dinner. | C M S | Before dinner. |
| | C M T | After dinner. |
| Dismasted. | C M V | A dismasted Vessel reported at *place indicated.* |
| | C M W | Go to the assistance of dismasted Vessel. |

## SENTENCES.

### No Distinguishing Flag.

| Leading Words. | Letters. | D |
|---|---|---|
| Dismasted. | C N B | Vessel seen is dismasted. |
| Distress. | C N D | *Vessel indicated* is in distress. |
| | C N F | Ascertain nature of Vessel in distress, and assist her if required. |
| | C N G | I am in great distress, and require immediate assistance. |
| | C N H | What is the nature of your distress? |
| | C N J | If you are in great distress and require immediate assistance, show ensign in mizen rigging. |
| | C N K | If you are in great distress and require immediate assistance, show blue lights at intervals. |
| Doctor. | C N L | Doctor required immediately. |
| | C N M | Doctor required with surgical instruments. |
| | C N P | Doctor required when we communicate. |
| | C N Q | Have you the Doctor on board? |
| | C N R | Doctor is on board of *Vessel indicated*. |
| | C N S | Doctor's services no longer required. |
| | C N T | Ship *No. indicated* requires a Doctor. |
| | C N V | Doctor declines going; too much sea. |
| | C N W | Doctor declines going; reasons will not state. |

## SENTENCES.

### No Distinguishing Flag.

| LEADING WORDS. | LETTERS. | D |
|---|---|---|
| Doctor. | C P B | Doctor is ill, and unable to come. |
| | C P D | No Doctor at the Station. |
| Draft. | C P F | What is your draft ? |
| | C P G | My draft is *as indicated*. |
| | C P H | Are you above or below the established draft ? |
| | C P J | I am above the established draft. |
| | C P K | I am below the established draft. |
| | C P L | I am the established draft. |
| | C P M | What is the draft of *Vessel indicated* ? |
| | C P N | The draft of *Vessel indicated* is *as indicated*. |
| Drop. | C P Q | Drop under my stern. |
| | C P R | Dropped foul of vessel. |
| | C P S | You can drop down to *place indicated*. |
| | C P T | I shall drop down to *place indicated*. |
| | C P V | Dropped past during the night. |
| | C P W | |

# PART V.

## SENTENCES.

### No Distinguishing Flag.

| LEADING WORDS. | LETTERS. | D |
|---|---|---|
| | C Q B | |
| | C Q D | |
| | C Q F | |
| | C Q G | |
| | C Q H | |
| | C Q J | |
| | C Q K | |

Q

# PART V.

## SENTENCES.

### No Distinguishing Flag.

| Leading Words. | Letters. | E |
|---|---|---|
| **Electric Telegraph.** | **C Q L** | Communicate without delay by Electric Telegraph to Master Attendant *the following message*—Vessel waiting for steam. |
| | **C Q M** | Communicate without delay by Electric Telegraph to Master Attendant *the following message*—Vessel dismasted. |
| | **C Q N** | Communicate without delay by Electric Telegraph to Master Attendant *the following message*—Vessel leaky. |
| | **C Q P** | Communicate without delay by Electric Telegraph to Master Attendant *the following message*—Vessel crew mutinied. |
| | **C Q R** | Communicate without delay by Electric Telegraph to Master Attendant *the following message*—Vessel burnt. |

NOTE.—In using the signals commencing with C Q L and ending with C S D, the Vessel's name to which the signal refers is in all cases to follow.

# PART V.

## SENTENCES.

### No Distinguishing Flag.

| Leading Words. | Letters. | E |
|---|---|---|
| Electric Telegraph. | C Q S | Communicate without delay by Electric Telegraph to Master Attendant *the following message*—Vessel lost. |
| | C Q T | Communicate without delay by Electric Telegraph to Master Attendant *the following message*—Vessel aground. |
| | C Q V | Communicate without delay by Electric Telegraph to Master Attendant *the following message*—Vessel been in collision. |
| | C Q W | Communicate without delay by Electric Telegraph to Master Attendant *the following message*—Vessel waiting for Pilot. |

# PART V.

## SENTENCES.

### No Distinguishing Flag.

| LEADING WORDS. | LETTERS. | E |
|---|---|---|
| Electric Telegraph. | C R B | Communicate without delay by Electric Telegraph to Master Attendant *the following message*—Vessel broken windlass. |
| | C R D | Communicate without delay by Electric Telegraph to Master Attendant *the following message*—Vessel broken hawse pipes. |
| | C R F | Communicate without delay by Electric Telegraph to Master Attendant *the following message*—Vessel broken capstan. |
| | C R G | Communicate without delay by Electric Telegraph to Master Attendant *the following message*—Vessel waiting for anchors. |
| | C R H | Communicate without delay by Electric Telegraph to Master Attendant *the following message*—Vessel waiting for cables. |
| | C R J | Communicate without delay by Electric Telegraph to Master Attendant *the following message*—Vessel waiting for anchors and cables. |
| | C R K | Communicate without delay by Electric Telegraph to Master Attendant *the following message*—Vessel neaped. |
| | C R L | Communicate without delay by Electric Telegraph to Master Attendant *the following message*—Vessel crew sick. |

# PART V.

## SENTENCES.

### No Distinguishing Flag.

| Leading Words. | Letters. | E |
|---|---|---|
| **Electric Telegraph.** | **C R M** | Communicate without delay by Electric Telegraph to Master Attendant *the following message*—Vessel has plague on board. |
| | **C R N** | Communicate without delay by Electric Telegraph to Master Attendant *the following message*—Vessel wanting water. |
| | **C R P** | Communicate without delay by Electric Telegraph to Master Attendant *the following message*—Vessel wanting provisions. |
| | **C R Q** | Communicate without delay by Electric Telegraph to Master Attendant *the following message*—Vessel wanting coals. |
| | **C R S** | Communicate without delay by Electric Telegraph to Master Attendant *the following message*—Vessel wanting steam tug and cargo boats. |
| | **C R T** | Communicate without delay by Electric Telegraph to Master Attendant *the following message*—Vessel rudder gone. |
| | **C R V** | Communicate without delay by Electric Telegraph to Master Attendant *the following message*—Cyclone rapidly approaching Calcutta. |
| | **C R W** | Communicate without delay by Electric Telegraph to Master Attendant *the following message*—Pilot sick. |

# PART V.

## SENTENCES.

### No Distinguishing Flag.

| Leading Words. | Letters. | E |
|---|---|---|
| **Electric Telegraph.** | C S B | Communicate without delay by Electric Telegraph to Master Attendant *the following message*—Pilot dead. |
| | C S D | Communicate without delay by Electric Telegraph to Master Attendant *the following message*—Pilot drowned. |
| | C S F | Communicate without delay by Electric Telegraph to Master Attendant *the following message*—Commander dead. |
| | C S G | Communicate without delay by Electric Telegraph to Master Attendant *the following message*—Officers wanted at the cruizing station. |
| | C S H | Communicate without delay by Electric Telegraph to Master Attendant *the following message*—No Officers at the cruizing station. |
| | C S J | Communicate without delay by Electric Telegraph to Master Attendant *the following message*—Ships waiting for Pilots at cruizing station. |
| | C S K | Communicate without delay by Electric Telegraph to Master Attendant *the following message*—Ridge Light wants anchors. |
| | C S L | Communicate without delay by Electric Telegraph to Master Attendant *the following message*—Ridge Light wants cables. |

# PART V.

## SENTENCES.

### No Distinguishing Flag.

| Leading Words. | Letters. | E |
|---|---|---|
| Electric Telegraph. | C S M | Communicate without delay by Electric Telegraph to Master Attendant *the following message*—Ridge Light wants anchors and cables. |
| | C S N | Communicate without delay by Electric Telegraph to Master Attendant *the following message*—Ridge Light bolwn off the station. |
| | C S P | Communicate without delay by Electric Telegraph to Master Attendant *the following message*—Eastern Channel Light wants anchors. |
| | C S Q | Communicate without delay by Electric Telegraph to Master Attendant *the following message*—Eastern Channel Light wants cables. |
| | C S R | Communicate without delay by Electric Telegraph to Master Attendant *the following message*—Eastern Channel Light wants anchors and cables. |
| | C S T | Communicate without delay by Electric Telegraph to Master Attendant *the following message*—Eastern Channel Light blown off the station. |
| | C S V | Communicate without delay by Electric Telegraph to Master Attendant *the following message*—Lower Gasper Light wants anchors. |
| | C S W | Communicate without delay by Electric Telegraph to Master Attendant *the following message*—Lower Gasper Light wants cables. |

# PART V.

## SENTENCES.

### No Distinguishing Flag.

| LEADING WORDS. | LETTERS. | E |
|---|---|---|
| **Electric Telegraph.** | C T B | Communicate without delay by Electric Telegraph to Master Attendant *the following message*—Lower Gasper Light wants anchors and cables. |
| | C T D | Communicate without delay by Electric Telegraph to Master Attendant *the following message*—Lower Gasper Light blown off the station. |
| | C T F | Communicate without delay by Electric Telegraph to Master Attendant *the following message*—I have taken the Ridge Light Station. |
| | C T G | Communicate without delay by Electric Telegraph to Master Attendant *the following message*—I have taken the Eastern Channel Light Station. |
| | C T H | Communicate without delay by Electric Telegraph to Master Attendant *the following message*—I have taken the Lower Gasper Light Station. |
| | C T J | Communicate without delay by Electric Telegraph to Master Attendant *the following message*—I have taken the Upper Gasper Light Station. |
| | C T K | Communicate without delay by Electric Telegraph to Master Attendant *the following message*—Ridge Light missing. |
| | C T L | Communicate without delay by Electric Telegraph to Master Attendant *the following message*—Eastern Channel Light missing. |

NOTE.—In using the signals commencing with C T F and ending with C T J, the name of the Vessel to which the signal refers is in all cases to follow.

## SENTENCES.

### No Distinguishing Flag.

| Leading Words. | Letters. | E |
|---|---|---|
| Electric Telegraph. | C T M | Communicate without delay by Electric Telegraph to Master Attendant *the following message*—Lower Gasper Light missing. |
| | C T N | Communicate without delay by Electric Telegraph to Master Attendant *the following message*—Upper Gasper Light missing. |
| | C T P | Communicate without delay by Electric Telegraph to Master Attendant *the following message*—Pilot Vessels missing. |
| | C T Q | Communicate without delay by Electric Telegraph to Master Attendant *the following message*—Pilot Vessels not on station. |
| | C T R | Communicate without delay by Electric Telegraph to Master Attendant *the following message*—Pilot Vessels blown off station. |
| | C T S | Communicate your wants by Electric Telegraph. |
| | C T V | I have received a message for you by Electric Telegraph. |
| | C T W | Have you received any message for me by Electric Telegraph ? |

# PART V.

## SENTENCES.

### No Distinguishing Flag.

| Leading Words. | Letters. | E |
|---|---|---|
| End. | C V B | When does your cruize end ? |
| | C V D | My cruize ends on *date indicated*. |
| | C V F | Can you inform me when *vessel indicated* cruize ends ? |
| | C V G | *Vessel indicated* cruize ends on *date indicated* |
| Expected. | C V H | When do you expect *vessel or person indicated* ? |
| | C V J | *Vessel or person indicated* is expected on date *indicated*. |
| | C V K | Have you heard when the incoming English Mail Steamer is expected ? |
| | C V L | Incoming English Mail Steamer is expected on date *indicated*. |
| | C V M | I do not know when incoming English Mail Steamer is expected. |
| | C V N | |
| | C V P | |
| | C V Q | |

# PART V.

## SENTENCES.

### No Distinguishing Flag.

| Leading Words. | Letters. | F |
|---|---|---|
| Fathoms. | C V R | How many fathoms are you laying in ? |
| | C V S | I am laying in fathoms *as indicated*. |
| February. | C V T | February. |
| Feet. | C V W | How many feet did you carry across *place indicated?* |

| Leading Words. | Letters. | F |
|---|---|---|
| **Feet.** | **C W B** | I carried feet *indicated* across *place indicated.* |
| | **C W D** | How many feet shall I find across *place indicated ?* |
| | **C W F** | You will find across at low water feet *indicated.* |
| | **C W G** | You will find across now feet *indicated.* |
| | **C W H** | How many feet will there be at low water at *place indicated ?* |
| | **C W J** | How many feet will there be at high water at *place indicated ?* |
| | **C W K** | There will be at low water at *place indicated,* feet *indicated.* |
| | **C W L** | There will be at high water at *place indicated,* feet *indicated.* |
| | **C W M** | How many feet will there be on upper bar or ridge at low water to-day ? |
| | **C W N** | How many feet will there be on centre bar or ridge at low water to-day ? |
| | **C W P** | How many feet will there be on lower bar or ridge at low water to-day ? |
| | **C W Q** | There will be on upper bar or ridge feet *as indicated.* |
| | **C W R** | There will be on centre bar or ridge feet *as indicated.* |
| | **C W S** | There will be on lower bar or ridge feet *as indicated.* |
| | **C W T** | What will be the rise in feet to-day ? |
| | **C W V** | What will be the fall in feet to-day ? |

# PART V.

## SENTENCES.

### No Distinguishing Flag.

| Leading Words. | Letters. | F |
|---|---|---|
| Fire. | D B C | Assist the vessel on fire with men and means as quickly as possible. |
| | D B F | *Vessel indicated* is on fire. |
| | D B G | A vessel on fire bearing *as indicated*. |
| | D B H | My vessel is on fire, send men and means to our assistance as quickly as possible. |
| Flags. | D B J | Your flags do not blow clear. |
| Floating Light. | D B K | I will take the Floating Light Station in Eastern Channel. |
| | D B L | Will you take the Floating Light Station in Eastern Channel? |
| | D B M | Do not leave the Floating Light Station in Eastern Channel. |
| | D B N | The Floating Light in Eastern Channel will not leave her station. |
| | D B P | The Floating Light in Eastern Channel must not leave her station. |
| | D B Q | The Floating Light in Eastern Channel cannot leave her station. |
| | D B R | Is the Floating Light in Eastern Channel on her station? |
| | D B S | The Floating Light in Eastern Channel is on her station. |
| | D B T | The Floating Light in Eastern Channel is not on her station *date indicated*. |
| | D B V | The Floating Light in Eastern Channel will leave her station *date indicated*. |
| | D B W | The Floating Light in Eastern Channel will take her station on *date indicated*. |

*First*

## SENTENCES.

### No Distinguishing Flag.

| Leading Words. | Letters. | F |
|---|---|---|
| Floating Light Eastern Channel. | D C B | Supply Floating Light in Eastern Channel with any stores she requires. |
| | D C F | Proceed to Floating Light in Eastern Channel for lanthorn stores. |
| | D C G | Communicate with Floating Light in Eastern Channel, on your way in or out. |
| | D C H | Supply Floating Light in Eastern Channel with anchors. |
| | D C J | Supply Floating Light in Eastern Channel with cables. |
| | D C K | Supply Floating Light in Eastern Channel with anchors and cables. |
| | D C L | I have stores for Floating Light in Eastern Channel. |
| | D C M | Take from Floating Light in Eastern Channel any pilots on board. |
| | D C N | Take from Floating Light in Eastern Channel empty blue light barrels. |
| | D C P | I have private stores for Floating Light in Eastern Channel. |
| | D C Q | I have public stores for Floating Light in Eastern Channel. |
| | D C R | I have letters *private* for Floating Light in Eastern Channel. |
| | D C S | I have letters *public* for Floating Light in Eastern Channel. |
| | D C T | I have Commander of Floating Light in Eastern Channel on board. |
| | D C V | I have Chief Officer of Floating Light in Eastern Channel on board. |
| | D C W | I have Second Officer of Floating Light in Eastern Channel on board. |

# PART V.

## SENTENCES.

### No Distinguishing Flag.

| Leading Words. | Letters. | F |
|---|---|---|
| Floating Light Eastern Channel. | D F B | I have Crew of Floating Light in Eastern Channel on board. |
| | D F C | Floating Light in Eastern Channel wants anchors. |
| | D F G | Floating Light in Eastern Channel wants cables. |
| | D F H | Floating Light in Eastern Channel wants anchors and cables. |
| | D F J | Floating Light in Eastern Channel wants blue light composition. |
| | D F K | Floating Light in Eastern Channel wants lanthorn stores. |
| | D F L | Floating Light in Eastern Channel wants water. |
| | D F M | Floating Light in Eastern Channel wants provisions. |
| | D F N | Floating Light in Eastern Channel Crew are sick. |
| | D F P | Commander of Floating Light in Eastern Channel is sick. |
| | D F Q | Commander of Floating Light in Eastern Channel is dead. |
| | D F R | Chief Officer of Floating Light in Eastern Channel is sick. |
| | D F S | Chief Officer of Floating Light in Eastern Channel is dead. |
| | D F T | Second Officer of Floating Light in Eastern Channel is sick. |
| | D F V | Second Officer of Floating Light in Eastern Channel is dead. |
| | D F W | Floating Light in Eastern Channel has been blown off her station. |

# PART V.

## SENTENCES.

### No Distinguishing Flag.

| Leading Words. | Letters. | F |
|---|---|---|
| Foating Light Eastern. Channel. Floating Light Gasper Channel Lower. | D G B | Floating Light in Eastern Channel requires Doctor. |
| | D G C | I will take the Floating Light Lower Station in Gasper Channel. |
| | D G F | Will you take the Floating Light Lower Station in Gasper Channel? |
| | D G H | Do not leave the Floating Light Lower Station in Gasper Channel. |
| | D G J | Floating Light in Gasper Channel Lower, will not leave her station. |
| | D G K | Floating Light in Gasper Channel Lower must not leave her station. |
| | D G L | Floating Light in Gasper Channel Lower cannot leave her station. |
| | D G M | Floating Light in Gasper Channel Lower has been blown off her station. |
| | D G N | Floating Light in Gasper Channel Lower requires Doctor. |
| | D G P | Floating Light in Gasper Channel Lower wants anchors. |
| | D G Q | Floating Light in Gasper Channel Lower wants cables. |
| | D G R | Floating Light in Gasper Channel Lower wants anchors and cables. |
| | D G S | Floating Light in Gasper Channel Lower wants blue light composition. |
| | D G T | Floating Light in Gasper Channel Lower wants lanthorn stores. |
| | D G V | Floating Light in Gasper Channel Lower wants water. |
| | D G W | Floating Light in Gasper Channel Lower wants proviions. |

# PART V.

## SENTENCES.

### No Distinguishing Flag.

| LEADING WORDS. | LETTERS. | F |
|---|---|---|
| **Floating Light Gasper Channel Lower.** | D H B | Floating Light in Gasper Channel Lower Crew are sick. |
| | D H C | Is the Floating Light in Gasper Channel Lower on her station ? |
| | D H F | The Floating Light in Gasper Channel Lower is on her station. |
| | D H G | The Floating Light in Gasper Channel Lower is not on her station. |
| | D H J | The Floating Light in Gasper Channel Lower will leave her station on *date indicated.* |
| | D H K | The Floating Light in Gasper Channel Lower will take her station on *date indicated.* |
| | D H L | Supply Floating Light in Gasper Channel Lower with any stores she may require. |
| | D H M | Supply Floating Light in Gasper Channel Lower with anchors. |
| | D H N | Supply Floating Light in Gasper Channel Lower with cables. |
| | D H P | Supply Floating Light in Gasper Channel Lower with anchors and cables. |
| | D H Q | Proceed to Floating Light in Gasper Channel Lower for lanthorn stores. |
| | D H R | Communicate with Floating Light in Gasper Channel Lower on your way in or out. |
| | D H S | Take from Floating Light in Gasper Channel Lower empty blue light barrels. |
| | D H T | I have private stores for Floating Light in Gasper Channel Lower. |
| | D H V | I have public stores for Floating Light in Gasper Channel Lower. |
| | D H W | I have private letters for Floating Light in Gasper Channel Lower. |

s

# PART V.

## SENTENCES.

### No Distinguishing Flag.

| Leading Words. | Letters. | F |
|---|---|---|
| Floating Light Gasper Channel Lower. | D J B | I have public letters for Floating Light in Gasper Channel Lower. |
| | D J C | I have Commander of Floating Light in Gasper Channel Lower on board. |
| | D J F | I have Chief Officer of Floating Light in Gasper Channel Lower on board. |
| | D J G | I have Second Officer of Floating Light in Gasper Channel Lower on board. |
| | D J H | I have Crew of Floating Light in Gasper Channel Lower on board. |
| | D J K | Commander of Floating Light in Gasper Channel Lower is sick. |
| | D J L | Commander of Floating Light in Gasper Channel Lower is dead. |
| | D J M | Chief Officer of Floating Light in Gasper Channel Lower is sick. |
| | D J N | Chief Officer of Floating Light in Gasper Channel Lower is dead. |
| | D J P | Second Officer of Floating Light in Gasper Channel Lower is sick. |
| | D J Q | Second Officer of Floating Light in Gasper Channel Lower is dead. |
| Floating Light Gasper Channel Upper. | D J R | I will take the Floating Light Upper Station in Gasper Channel. |
| | D J S | Will you take the Floating Light Upper Station in Gasper Channel ? |
| | D J T | Do not leave the Floating Light Upper Station in Gasper Channel. |
| | D J V | Floating Light in Gasper Channel Upper will not leave her station. |
| | D J W | Floating Light in Gasper Channel Upper must not leave her station. |

## SENTENCES.

### No Distinguishing Flag.

| Leading Words. | Letters. | F |
|---|---|---|
| **Floating Light Gasper Channel Upper.** | **D K B** | Floating Light in Gasper Channel Upper cannot leave her station. |
| | **D K C** | Floating Light in Gasper Channel Upper has been blown off her station. |
| | **D K F** | Floating Light in Gasper Channel Upper wants Doctor. |
| | **D K G** | Floating Light in Gasper Channel Upper wants anchors. |
| | **D K H** | Floating Light in Gasper Channel Upper wants cables. |
| | **D K J** | Floating Light in Gasper Channel Upper wants anchors and cables. |
| | **D K L** | Floating Light in Gasper Channel Upper wants lanthorn stores. |
| | **D K M** | Floating Light in Gasper Channel Upper wants water. |
| | **D K N** | Floating Light in Gasper Channel Upper wants provisions. |
| | **D K P** | Floating Light in Gasper Channel Upper Crew are sick. |
| | **D K Q** | Is Floating Light in Gasper Channel Upper on her station? |
| | **D K R** | Floating Light in Gasper Channel Upper is on her station. |
| | **D K S** | Floating Light in Gasper Channel Upper is not on her station. |
| | **D K T** | Floating Light in Gasper Channel Upper will leave her station on *date indicated.* |
| | **D K V** | Floating Light in Gasper Channel Upper will take her station on *date indicated.* |
| | **D K W** | Supply Floating Light in Gasper Channel Upper with any stores she may require. |

# PART V.

—

## SENTENCES.

### No Distinguishing Flag.

| LEADING WORDS. | LETTERS. | F |
|---|---|---|
| Floating Light Gasper Channel Upper. | D L B | Supply Floating Light in Gasper Channel Upper with anchors. |
| | D L C | Supply Floating Light in Gasper Channel Upper with cables. |
| | D L F | Supply Floating Light in Gasper Channel Upper with anchors and cables. |
| | D L G | Communicate with Floating Light Gasper Channel Upper on your way in or out. |
| | D L H | I have private stores for Floating Light Gasper Channel Upper. |
| | D L J | I have public stores for Floating Light Gasper Channel Upper. |
| | D L K | I have private letters for Floating Light Gasper Channel Upper. |
| | D L M | I have public letters for Floating Light Gasper Channel Upper. |
| | D L N | I have Commander of Floating Light Gasper Channel Upper on board. |
| | D L P | I have Chief Officer of Floating Light Gasper Channel Upper on board. |
| | D L Q | I have Second Officer of Floating Light Gasper Channel Upper on board. |
| | D L R | I have Crew of Floating Light Gasper Channel Upper on board. |
| | D L S | Commander of Floating Light Gasper Channel Upper is sick. |
| | D L T | Commander of Floating Light Gasper Channel Upper is dead. |
| | D L V | Chief Officer of Floating Light Gasper Channel Upper is sick. |
| | D L W | Chief Officer of Floating Light Gasper Channel Upper is dead. |

## SENTENCES.

### No Distinguishing Flag.

| Leading Words. | Letters. | F |
|---|---|---|
| Floating Light Gasper Channel Upper. | D M B | Second Officer of Floating Light Gasper Channel Upper is sick. |
| | D M C | Second Officer of Floating Light Gasper Channel Upper is dead. |
| Floating Light Pilot's Ridge. | D M F | I will take the Floating Light Station on Pilot's Ridge. |
| | D M G | Will you take the Floating Light Station on Pilot's Ridge ? |
| | D M H | Do not leave the Floating Light Station on Pilot's Ridge. |
| | D M J | Floating Light on Pilot's Ridge will not leave her station. |
| | D M K | Floating Light on Pilot's Ridge must not leave her station. |
| | D M L | Floating Light on Pilot's Ridge cannot leave her station. |
| | D M N | Floating Light on Pilot's Ridge has been blown off her station. |
| | D M P | Floating Light on Pilot's Ridge requires Doctor. |
| | D M Q | Floating Light on Pilot's Ridge requires anchors. |
| | D M R | Floating Light on Pilot's Ridge requires cables. |
| | D M S | Floating Light on Pilot's Ridge requires anchors and cables. |
| | D M T | Floating Light on Pilot's Ridge requires blue light composition. |
| | D M V | Floating Light on Pilot's Ridge requires lanthorn stores. |
| | D M W | Floating Light on Pilot's Ridge requires water. |

# PART V.

## SENTENCES.

### No Distinguishing Flag.

| Leading Words. | Letters. | F |
|---|---|---|
| **Floating Light Pilot's Ridge.** | D N B | Floating Light on Pilot's Ridge requires provisions. |
| | D N C | Floating Light on Pilot's Ridge Crew are sick. |
| | D N F | Is the Floating Light on Pilot's Ridge on her station ? |
| | D N G | The Floating Light on Pilot's Ridge is on her station. |
| | D N H | The Floating Light on Pilot's Ridge is not on her station. |
| | D N J | The Floating Light on Pilot's Ridge will take her station on *date indicated.* |
| | D N K | The Floating Light on Pilot's Ridge will leave her station on *date indicated.* |
| | D N L | Supply Floating Light on Pilot's Ridge with what stores she may require. |
| | D N M | Supply Floating Light on Pilot's Ridge with anchors. |
| | D N P | Supply Floating Light on Pilot's Ridge with cables. |
| | D N Q | Supply Floating Light on Pilot's Ridge with anchors and cables. |
| | D N R | Proceed to Floating Light on Pilot's Ridge for lanthorn stores. |
| | D N S | Communicate with Floating Light on Pilot's Ridge as soon as possible. |
| | D N T | Take from Floating Light on Pilot's Ridge empty blue light barrels. |
| | D N V | I have private stores for Floating Light on Pilot's Ridge. |
| | D N W | I have public stores for Floating Light on Pilot's Ridge. |

# PART V.

## SENTENCES.

### No Distinguishing Flag.

| LEADING WORDS. | LETTERS. | F |
|---|---|---|
| Floating Light Pilot's Ridge. | D P B | I have private letters for Floating Light on Pilot's Ridge. |
| | D P C | I have public letters for Floating Light on Pilot's Ridge. |
| | D P F | I have Commander of Floating Light on Pilot's Ridge on board. |
| | D P G | I have Chief Officer of Floating Light on Pilot's Ridge on board. |
| | D P H | I have Second Officer of Floating Light on Pilot's Ridge on board. |
| | D P J | I have Crew of Floating Light on Pilot's Ridge on board. |
| | D P K | Commander of Floating Light on Pilot's Ridge is sick. |
| | D P L | Commander of Floating Light on Pilot's Ridge is dead. |
| | D P M | Chief Officer of Floating Light on Pilot's Ridge is sick. |
| | D P N | Chief Officer of Floating Light on Pilot's Ridge is dead. |
| | D P Q | Second Officer of Floating Light on Pilot's Ridge is sick. |
| | D P R | Second Officer of Floating Light on Pilot's Ridge is dead. |
| Fore. | D P S | I have badly sprung my fore-mast. |
| | D P T | I have badly sprung my fore-topmast. |
| | D P V | I have badly sprung my fore-yard. |
| | D P W | I have badly sprung my lower fore-topsail yard. |

## SENTENCES.

### No Distinguishing Flag.

| LEADING WORDS. | LETTERS. | F |
|---|---|---|
| **Fore.** | D Q B | I have badly sprung my upper fore-topsail yard. |
| | D Q C | My or *Vessel indicated* fore-mast is rotten. |
| | D Q F | My or *Vessel indicated* fore-topmast is rotten. |
| | D Q G | My or *Vessel indicated* fore-yard is rotten. |
| | D Q H | My or *Vessel indicated* lower fore-topsail yard is rotten. |
| | D Q J | My or *Vessel indicated* upper fore-topsail yard is rotten. |
| | D Q K | My or *Vessel indicated* fore-yard is carried away. |
| | D Q L | My or *Vessel indicated* lower fore-topsail yard is carried away. |
| | D Q M | My or *Vessel indicated* upper fore-topsail yard is carried away. |
| **Forms.** | D Q N | Can you supply me with forms blank ? |
| | D Q P | I will supply you with forms blank. |
| | D Q R | *Friday* |
| | D Q S | *Fourth* |
| | D Q T | *Fifth* |
| | D Q V | *Fourteent Fifteenth* |
| | D Q W | *Four teenth —* |

# PART V.

## SENTENCES.

### No Distinguishing Flag.

| Leading Words. | Letters. | F |
|---|---|---|
| | D R B | |
| | D R C | |
| | D R F | |
| | D R G | |
| | D R H | |

# PART V.

## SENTENCES.

### No Distinguishing Flag.

| Leading Words. | Letters. | G |
|---|---|---|
| Gale. | D R J | Prepare for a gale. |
| | D R K | There is every indication of a gale. |
| | D R L | You are not in a good position for riding out a gale. |
| | D R M | I have experienced a heavy gale from *quarter indicated.* |
| | D R N | Has the recent gale caused you any damage ? |
| | D R P | State damage sustained in gale. |
| | D R Q | |
| | D R S | |
| | D R T | |
| | D R V | |
| | D R W | |

# PART V.

## SENTENCES.

### No Distinguishing Flag.

| Leading Words. | Letters. | H |
|---|---|---|
| Hail. | D S B | Come within hail |
| | D S C | I shall not fetch within hail unless you trip your anchor. |
| | D S F | If you wish me to pass within hail bear down to me. |
| Hawser. | D S G | Send me the end of your hawser. |
| | D S H | I will send you the end of my hawser. |
| Hour. | D S J | At what hour ? |
| | D S K | One A. M. |
| | D S L | Two A. M. |
| | D S M | Three A. M. |
| | D S N | Four A. M. |
| | D S P | Five A. M. |
| | D S Q | Six A. M. |
| | D S R | Seven A. M. |
| | D S T | Eight A. M. |
| | D S V | Nine A. M. |
| | D S W | Ten A. M. |

# PART V.

—

## SENTENCES.

### No Distinguishing Flag.

| LEADING WORDS. | LETTERS. | H |
|---|---|---|
| Hour. | D T B | Eleven A. M. |
| | D T C | Noon. |
| | D T F | One P. M. |
| | D T G | Two P. M. |
| | D T H | Three P. M. |
| | D T J | Four P. M. |
| | D T K | Five P. M. |
| | D T L | Six P. M. |
| | D T M | Seven P. M. |
| | D T N | Eight P. M. |
| | D T P | Nine P. M. |
| | D T Q | Ten P. M. |
| | D T R | Eleven P. M. |
| | D T S | Midnight. |
| | D T V | |
| | D T W | |

# PART V.

## SENTENCES.

### No Distinguishing Flag.

| LEADING WORDS. | LETTERS. | H |
|---|---|---|
| | D V B | |
| . | D V C | |
| | D V F | |

| Leading Words. | Letters. | |
|---|---|---|
| Inability. | D V G | Inability. |
| | D V H | What is the cause of your inability ? |
| Information. | D V J | Have you any information of *person* or *Vessel indicated ?* |
| | D V K | Have you any information when we may expect English Mail Steamer ? |
| | D V L | Have you any information when we may expect French Mail Steamer ? |
| | D V M | Have you any information when we may expect China Mail Steamer ? |
| | D V N | Have you any information when we may expect East Coast Mail Steamer ? |
| | D V P | Have you any information when we may expect West Coast Mail Steamer ? |
| | D V Q | |
| | D V R | |
| | D V S | |
| | D V T | |
| | D V W | |

# PART V.

## SENTENCES.

### No Distinguishing Flag.

| Leading Words. | Letters. | J |
|---|---|---|
| January. | D W B | January. |
| July. | D W C | July. |
| June. | D W F | June. |
| Junk Coir. | D W G | Can you spare me some junk coir ? |
| Junk Europe. | D W H | Can you spare me some junk Europe ? |
| | D W J | |
| | D W K | |
| | D W L | |

# PART V.

## SENTENCES.

### No Distinguishing Flag.

| LEADING WORDS. | LETTERS. | K |
|---|---|---|
| Keep. | D W M | Keep a Branch Pilot for *purpose indicated.* |
| | D W N | Keep a Brevet Branch Pilot for *purpose indicated.* |
| | D W P | Keep a Branch Pilot for English Mail. |
| | D W Q | Keep a Brevet Branch Pilot for English Mail. |
| | D W R | Keep a Senior Master Pilot for English Mail. |
| | D W S | Keep a Branch Pilot for French Mail. |
| | D W T | Keep a Brevet Branch Pilot for French Mail. |
| | D W V | Keep a Senior Master Pilot for French Mail. |

# PART V.

## SENTENCES.

### No Distinguishing Flag.

| LEADING WORDS. | LETTERS. | K |
|---|---|---|
| Keep. | F B C | Keep the Senior Branch Pilot for Line of Battle Ship. |
| | F B D | Keep the Senior Branch Pilot for first class Frigate. |
| | F B G | Keep the Senior Branch Pilot for H. M.'s Transport. |
| | F B H | Keep the Senior Branch Pilot for Vessel *as indicated* with Admiral on board. |
| | F B J | Keep the Senior Branch Pilot for Vessel *as indicated* with Commodore on board. |
| | F B K | Keep the Senior Branch Pilot for Vessel *as indicated* with Viceroy on board. |
| | F B L | Keep the Senior Branch Pilot for Vessel *as indicated* with a Prince on board. |
| | F B M | Keep Senior Officer for purpose *as indicated.* |
| Know. | F B N | Do you know ? |
| | F B P | I do not know. |
| | F B Q | |
| | F B R | |
| | F B S | |
| | F B T | |
| | F B V | |
| | F B W | |

# PART V.

## SENTENCES.

### No Distinguishing Flag.

| Leading Words. | Letters. | K |
|---|---|---|
| | F C B | |
| | F C D | |
| | F C G | |
| | F C H | |
| | F C J | |

# PART V.

## SENTENCES.

### No Distinguishing Flag.

| Leading Words. | Letters. | L |
|---|---|---|
| Lay to. | F C K | Lay to on starboard tack. |
| | F C L | Lay to on port tack. |
| | F C M | Lay to. |
| | F C N | Do not lay to ? |
| | F C P | Shall I lay to ? |
| | F C Q | Continue to lay to. |
| | F C R | Lay to ahead of me. |
| | F C S | Lay to astern of me. |
| | F C T | Lay to to windward of me. |
| | F C V | Lay to to leeward of me. |
| | F C W | I will lay to ahead of you. |

# PART V.

## SENTENCES.

### No Distinguishing Flag.

| LEADING WORDS. | LETTERS. | L |
|---|---|---|
| **Lay to.** | F D B | I will lay to astern of you. |
| | F D C | I will lay to to windward of you. |
| | F D G | I will lay to to leeward of you. |
| **Leadsman.** | F D H | Will you supply me with a Leadsman? |
| | F D J | I will supply you with a Leadsman. |
| | F D K | I cannot supply you with a Leadsman. |
| | F D L | *Vessel indicated* can supply you with a Leadsman. |
| | F D M | Supply *Vessel indicated* with a Leadsman |
| | F D N | My Leadsman is ill, will you give him a passage to Town? |
| | F D P | Shall I put my Leadsman on board as Pilot of *Vessel indicated?* |
| | F D Q | I have put my Leadsman on board as Pilot of *Vessel indicated.* |
| | F D R | Have you any Leadsman? |
| | F D S | Put your Leadsman as Pilot on board of *Vessel indicated.* |
| | F D T | No Leadsman on board. |
| | F D V | If Leadsman is competent, put him as Pilot on board of *Vessel indicated.* |
| **Leak.** | F D W | Vessel in sight has sprung a leak. |
| | | *Have you a leadman on board* |
| | | *I have a leadman "    "* |

# PART V.

## SENTENCES.

### No Distinguishing Flag.

| Leading Words. | Letters. | L |
|---|---|---|
| Leak. | F G B | *Vessel indicated* has sprung a leak. |
| | F G C | Vessel in sight is in a dangerously leaky condition. |
| | F G D | *Vessel indicated* is in a dangerously leaky condition. |
| | F G H | Leak increases and is dangerous. |
| | F G J | Vessel in sight is foundering from cause of leak. |
| | F G K | Vessel *indicated* is foundering from cause of leak. |
| | F G L | I have sprung a leak. |
| Leave. | F G M | When did or will *Vessel indicated* leave? |
| | F G N | *Vessel indicated* did or will leave on *date indicated*. |
| Letters. | F G P | Send for your letters. |
| | F G Q | I have letters for you. |
| | F G R | I have no letters for you. |
| | F G S | I will send you your letters. |
| | F G T | Will you take a letter for me ? |
| | F G V | Have you any letters for me ? |
| | F G W | There are letters on board of *Vessel indicated* for you. |

*[Vessel ind]/, wants a letter taken to him*

## SENTENCES.

### No Distinguishing Flag.

| Leading Words. | Letters. | L |
|---|---|---|
| Letters. | F H B | There are letters on board of *Vessel indicated* for you or *person indicated*. |
| | F H C | There are letters in the Dâk Boat for you. |
| | F H D | Shall I take your letters? |
| | F H G | I have letters for outward bound English Mail Steamer. |
| | F H J | I have letters for outward bound French Mail Steamer. |
| | F H K | I have letters for outward bound China Mail Steamer. |
| | F H L | I have letters for outward bound West Coast Mail Steamer. |
| | F H M | I have letters for outward bound East Coast Mail Steamer. |
| | F H N | I have letters for inward bound English Mail Steamer. |
| | F H P | I have letters for inward bound French Mail Steamer. |
| | F H Q | I have letters for inward bound China Mail Steamer. |
| | F H R | I have letters for inward bound West Coast Mail Steamer. |
| | F H S | I have letters for inward bound East Coast Mail Steamer. |
| | F H T | I have letters for *Vessel indicated*. |
| | F H V | I have a service letter for you. |
| | F H W | I have a service letter for *you* or *person indicated*. |

# PART V.

## SENTENCES.

### No Distinguishing Flag.

| LEADING WORDS. | LETTERS. | L |
|---|---|---|
| Letters. | F J B | Open all service letters to my address during my absence and act upon them. |
| | F J C | Have you any letters for England ? |
| | F J D | Have you any letters for Calcutta ? |
| | F J G | Be careful of letters, as they are of importance. |
| | F J H | All the letters have not been delivered. |
| | F J K | Wait for letters. |
| Licensed Pilots. | F J L | I have a licensed Branch Pilot on board. |
| | F J M | I have a licensed Master Pilot on board. |
| | F J N | I have a licensed Mate Pilot on board. |
| | F J P | I have a licensed Leadsman on board. |
| | F J Q | Can licensed Branch Pilot return to town ? |
| | F J R | Can licensed Master Pilot return to town ? |
| | F J S | Can licensed Mate Pilot return to town ? |
| | F J T | Can licensed Leadsman return to town ? |
| | F J V | Licensed Branch Pilot has a return order. |
| | F J W | Licensed Master Pilot has a return order. |

# PART V.

## SENTENCES.

### No Distinguishing Flag.

| LEADING WORDS. | LETTERS. | L |
|---|---|---|
| **Licensed Pilots.** | F K B | Licensed Mate Pilot has a return order. |
| | F K C | Licensed Leadsman has a return order. |
| | F K D | Licensed Branch Pilot may return. |
| | F K G | Licensed Branch Pilot's services cannot be spared. |
| | F K H | Licensed Master Pilot may return. |
| | F K J | Licensed Master Pilot's services cannot be spared. |
| | F K L | Licensed Mate Pilot may return. |
| | F K M | Licensed Mate Pilot's services cannot be spared. |
| | F K N | Licensed Leadsman may return. |
| | F K P | Licensed Leadsman's services cannot be spared. |
| | F K Q | What orders regarding licensed Branch Pilots ? |
| | F K R | What orders regarding licensed Master Pilots ? |
| | F K S | |
| | F K T | What orders regarding licensed Mate Pilots ? |
| | F K V | What orders regarding licensed Leadsman ? |
| | F K W | Put licensed Branch Pilot on board of *Vessel indicated.* |

## SENTENCES.

### No Distinguishing Flag.

| Leading Words. | Letters. | L |
|---|---|---|
| Licensed Pilots. | F L B | Put licensed Master Pilot on board of *Vessel indicated.* |
| | F L C | Put licensed Mate Pilot on board of *Vessel indicated.* |
| | F L D | Do not put licensed Branch Pilot on board of *Vessel indicated.* |
| | F L G | Do not put licensed Master Pilot on board of *Vessel indicated.* |
| | F L H | Do not put licensed Mate Pilot on board of *Vessel indicated.* |
| Light. | F L J | Show a light at night. |
| | F L K | Do not show a light. |
| | F L M | Shall I show a light ? |
| | F L N | Will you show a light ? |
| | F L P | I will show a light. |
| | F L Q | I will not show a light. |
| | F L R | I have not been able to show the usual lights during the night post. |
| | F L S | Shall I show the usual lights during the night ? |
| | F L T | Show the usual lights during the night. |
| | F L V | Do not show the usual lights. |
| | F L W | Will you show the usual lights ? |

| Leading Words. | Letters. | L |
|---|---|---|
| Light. | F M B | I will show the usual lights. |
| | F M C | I will not show the usual lights. |
| | F M D | I have not the means of showing the usual lights. |
| | F M G | Did you see any strange lights last night? |
| | F M H | I saw strange lights last night from *quarter indicated*. |
| | F M J | Show a light or lights at *position indicated* for my guidance during the night. |
| | F M K | I will show a light or lights at *place indicated* for your guidance during the night. |
| Look out. | F M L | Keep a good look out for *Vessel or person indicated*. |
| | F M N | Has a good look out been kept? |
| | F M P | A good look out has been kept. |
| | F M Q | A good look out has not been kept. |
| Lost. | F M R | A Vessel lost at or on *place indicated*. |
| | F M S | A Vessel reported to be lost at or on *place indicated*. |
| | F M T | A Vessel reported to be lost seen at *place indicated*. |
| Lump. | F M V | A lump has risen off *place indicated* No. of feet *indicated* at low water. |
| | F M W | The lump off *place indicated* has gone further to *direction indicated*. |

# PART V.

## SENTENCES.

### No Distinguishing Flag.

| Leading Words. | Letters. | L |
|---|---|---|
| Lump. | F N B | The lump off *place indicated* has disappeared. |
| | F N C | What water is there on the lump off *place indicated*? |
| | F N D | There are No. of feet *indicated* at low water at *place indicated*. |
| | F N G | It is very lumpy. |
| | F N H | |
| | F N J | |
| | F N K | |
| | F N L | |

## SENTENCES.

### No Distinguishing Flag.

| LEADING WORDS. | LETTERS. | M |
|---|---|---|
| Main. | F N M | I have badly sprung my main-mast. |
|  | F N P | I have badly sprung my main-yard. |
|  | F N Q | I have badly sprung my main-topmast. |
|  | F N R | I have badly sprung my main-topsail yard upper. |
|  | F N S | I have badly sprung my main-topsail yard lower. |
|  | F N T | My or *Vessel indicated* main-mast is rotten. |
|  | F N V | My or *Vessel indicated* main-yard is rotten. |
|  | F N W | My or *Vessel indicated* main-topmast is rotten. |

| LEADING WORDS. | LETTERS. | M |
|---|---|---|
| Main. | F P B | My or *Vessel indicated* main-topsail yard upper. |
| | F P C | My or *Vessel indicated* main-topsail yard lower. |
| Manœuvres. | F P D | Observe and follow my manœuvres. |
| | F P G | Pay no attention to my manœuvres. |
| | F P H | Follow the manœuvres of *Vessel indicated*. |
| | F P J | Pay no attention to the manœuvres of *Vessel indicated*. |
| Maroon. | F P K | Show a maroon every hour at night. |
| | F P L | Show a maroon every half hour at night. |
| | F P M | Show a maroon every quarter hour at night. |
| | F P N | I shall show a maroon every hour at night. |
| | F P Q | I shall show a maroon every half hour at night. |
| | F P R | I shall show a maroon every quarter hour at night. |
| | F P S | Show a maroon for my guidance on sighting light *as indicated* or striking soundings on *place indicated*. |
| March. | F P T | March. |
| Masts. | F P V | Masts, main. |
| | F P W | Masts, main-top. |

# PART V.

## SENTENCES.

### No Distinguishing Flag.

| Leading Words. | Letters. | M |
|---|---|---|
| Masts. | F Q B | Masts main-topgallant. |
| | F Q C | Masts main-royal. |
| | F Q D | Masts fore. |
| | F Q G | Masts foretop. |
| | F Q H | Masts foretop-gallant. |
| | F Q J | Masts fore-royal. |
| Master At-tendant. | F Q K | Master Attendant. |
| | F Q L | Deputy Master Attendant. |
| | F Q M | Inform Master Attendant *as indicated*. |
| May. | F Q N | May. |
| Morrow. | F Q P | To-morrow. |
| | F Q R | The day after to-morrow. |
| | F Q S | To-morrow morning. |
| | F Q T | *Monday* |
| | F Q V | |
| | F Q W | |

# PART V.

## SENTENCES.

### No Distinguishing Flag.

| Leading Words. | Letters. | N |
|---|---|---|
| News. | F R B | What news? |
| | F R C | Have you any news? |
| | F R D | No news. |
| | F R G | News is of importance. |
| | F R H | No important news. |
| Newspaper. | F R J | Have you a newspaper? |
| | F R K | I will send the newspaper. |
| | F R L | Can you send me a newspaper? |
| | F R M | What is the latest date of your newspaper? |
| | F R N | Send me the latest date of your newspaper. |
| Night. | F R P | At night. |
| | F R Q | Last night. |
| | F R S | To-night. |
| | F R T | To-morrow night. |
| | F R V | Night before last. |
| November. | F R W | November. |
| | | *Ninth* |
| | | *Nineteenth* |

# PART V.

## SENTENCES.

### No Distinguishing Flag.

| LEADING WORDS. | LETTERS. | N |
|---|---|---|
| Number. | F S B | Number. |
| | F S C | What number ? |
| | F S D | I require number *indicated*. |
| | F S G | |
| | F S H | |

## SENTENCES.

### No Distinguishing Flag.

| Leading Words. | Letters. | O |
|---|---|---|
| October. | F S J | October. |
| Officer's Accommodation. | F S K | What number of Officers can you accommodate? |
| | F S L | I can accommodate *No. indicated*. |
| | F S M | How many more Officers can you accommodate? |
| | F S N | I can accommodate *No. indicated*. |
| | F S P | I can accommodate all the Officers. |
| | F S Q | I cannot accommodate all the Officers. |
| | F S R | No more accommodation for Officers. |
| Officer's Aplication. | F S T | *Officer indicated* holds an application for a ship. |
| | F S V | The following Officers have given in applications for ships—*names to follow.* |
| | F S W | Can *Officer indicated* make use of his application? |

*State if officer indicated holds an application, or conditional return order,*

# PART V.

## SENTENCES.

### No Distinguishing Flag.

| Leading Words. | Letters. | O |
|---|---|---|
| Officer's Application. | F T B | *Officer indicated* can make use of his application. |
| | F T C | I cannot yet sanction the use of any applications. |
| | F T D | Not enough Officers to sanction use of application. |
| | F T C | *Officer indicated* cannot make use of his application. |
| | F T H | Wait further orders regarding application. |
| | F T J | I will send further orders regarding applications. |
| | F T K | Allow Officers to make use of applications according to priority of date. |
| | F T L | Allow Officers to make use of applications according to turn. |

# PART V.

## SENTENCES.

### No Distinguishing Flag.

| Leading Words. | Letters. | O |
|---|---|---|
| Officer's Application. | F T M | Use your own judgment as most beneficial to the Public Service in allowing Officers the benefit of applications. |
|  | F T N | May I allow *Officer indicated* to make use of his application ? |
| Officers Arrived. | F T P | Has *Officer indicated* arrived ? |
|  | F T Q | *Officer indicated* has arrived. |
|  | F T R | *Officer indicated* has not arrived. |
| Officers on Board. | F T S | Send on board *Officer indicated.* |
|  | F T V | Send *Officer or Officers indicated* on board of *Vessel indicated.* |
|  | F T W | Shall I send on board *Officer or Officers indicated ?* |

# PART V.

## SENTENCES.

### No Distinguishing Flag.

| LEADING WORDS. | LETTERS. | O |
|---|---|---|
| Officers Buoy Station Vessel. | F V B | What Officers are there on board Buoy Station Vessel ? |
| | F V C | There are no Officers on board of Buoy Station Vessel. |
| | F V D | There are Officers *as indicated* on board of Buoy Station Vessel. |
| | F V G | I have taken Officers *No. indicated* from Buoy Station Vessel. |
| | F V H | Put *Officers indicated* on board of Buoy Station Vessel. |
| | F V J | Put Officers *No. indicated* of last turn on board of Buoy Station Vessel. |
| | F V K | Shall I put the last turn Officers on board of Buoy Station Vessel ? |
| | F V L | Take all Officers from Buoy Station Vessel. |

# PART V.

## SENTENCES.

### No Distinguishing Flag.

| Leading Words. | Letters. | O |
|---|---|---|
| Officers Buoy Station Vessel. | F V M | Shall I take all Officers from Buoy Station Vessel ? |
| | F V N | Put all the Officers on board of Buoy Station Vessel. |
| | F V P | Shall I put all the Officers on board of Buoy Station Vessel ? |
| | F V Q | Take Officers from *Vessel indicated* and put them on board of Buoy Station Vessel. |
| | F V R | Take Officers from *Vessel indicated* and place one-third with the last turns on board of Buoy Station Vessel. |
| | F V S | Put Officers one-third with the last turns on board of Buoy Station Vessel, remainder put on Cruizing Vessel. |
| | F V T | Put Officers one-third with the last turns on board of Buoy Station Vessel, remainder divide as follows—first turns one-third on board of Cruizer, remainder intermediate. |
| | F V W | Put Officers one-third with the last turns on board of Buoy Station Vessel, send me the remainder. |

| Leading Words. | Letters. | O |
|---|---|---|
| Officer Chief. | F W B | Chief Officer. |
| | F W C | Have you my Chief Officer on board ? |
| | F W D | I have your Chief Officer on board. |
| | F W G | I have not your Chief Officer on board. |
| | F W H | Send your Chief Officer on board. |
| | F W J | Do you know if my Chief Officer is on his way down ? |
| | F W K | I have been compelled to put my Chief Officer on board of a Vessel. |
| | F W L | I have been compelled to send my Chief Officer to town. |
| | F W M | I am without a Chief Officer. |
| | F W N | I am without news of your Chief Officer. |
| | F W P | My Chief Officer is ill. |
| | F W Q | My Chief Officer is drowned. |
| | F W R | My Chief Officer is dead. |
| | F W S | My Chief Officer is too ill to remain on board any longer. |
| | F W T | My Chief Officer is dangerously ill. |
| | F W V | Your Chief Officer is on his way down. |

# PART V.

## SENTENCES.

### No Distinguishing Flag.

| Leading Words. | Letters. | O |
|---|---|---|
| Officer Chief. | G B C | You may expect your Chief Officer in *Vessel indicated*. |
| | G B D | I will relieve your Chief Officer. |
| | G B F | I cannot relieve your Chief Officer. |
| | G B H | Can you relieve my Chief Officer ? |
| Officers Coming Out. | G B J | I have come out with Officers. |
| | G B K | I have come out for Officers or *Officer indicated*. |
| | G B L | *Vessel indicated* has come out for Officers. |
| | G B M | *Vessel indicated* has come out with Officers. |
| | G B N | Officers are coming down in *Vessel indicated*. |
| | G B P | Have any Officers come out during the night ? |
| | G B Q | Name the Officers come out during my absence. |
| | G B R | Officers are coming down to Station. |
| Officers Competent. | G B S | Have you any competent Officers on board ? |
| | G B T | I have competent Officers on board. |
| | G B V | I have no competent Officers on board. |
| | G B W | Send a competent Officer on board of *Vessel indicated*. |

# PART V.

## SENTENCES.

### No Distinguishing Flag.

| Leading Words. | Letters. | O |
|---|---|---|
| **Officers Competent.** | G C B | Send me a competent Officer on survey duty. |
| | G C D | Send me a competent Officer for duty *indicated*. |
| | G C F | Send a competent Officer to relieve Commander of *Vessel indicated*. |
| | G C H | Send a competent Officer to relieve Chief Officer of *Vessel indicated*. |
| | G C J | Send a competent Officer to relieve Second Officer of *Vessel indicated*. |
| | G C K | I will send you a competent Officer for duty *indicated*. |
| | G C L | I have no competent Officer for duty *indicated*. |
| | G C M | I have no competent Officer for survey duty. |

# PART V.

## SENTENCES,

### No Distinguishing Flag.

| Leading Words. | Letters. | O |
|---|---|---|
| **Officers Cruizing Station.** | G C N | What Officers are there at the Cruizing Station. |
| | G C P | There are Officers *as indicated* at the Cruizing Station. |
| | G C Q | There are no Officers at the Cruizing Station. |
| | G C R | I have Officers on board for the Cruizing Station. |
| | G C S | I have no Officers on board for the Cruizing Station. |
| | G C T | Proceed with Officers to the Cruizing Station. |
| | G C V | Officers are on their way down to the Cruizing Station. |
| | G C W | Have you any Officers for the Cruizing Station ? |

# PART V.

## SENTENCES.

### No Distinguishing Flag.

| Leading Words. | Letters. | O |
|---|---|---|
| Officers Cruizing Station. | G D B | Desire the first Officer going up to report the want of Officers at the Cruizing Station to Master Attendant by Electric Telegraph. |
| | G D C | I have come from the Cruizing Station for Officers. |
| Vessel. | G D F | What Officers are there on board of Cruizing Station Vessel ? |
| | G D H | There are no Officers on board of Cruizing Station Vessel. |
| | G D J | There are Officers *as indicated* on board of Cruizing Station Vessel. |
| | G D K | I have taken Officers *as indicated* from Cruizing Station Vessel. |
| | G D L | Put Officers *as indicated* on board of Cruizing Station Vessel. |
| | G D M | Put Officers *No. indicated* of first turn on board of Cruizing Station Vessel. |

# PART V.

## SENTENCES.

### No Distinguishing Flag.

| LEADING WORDS. | LETTERS. | O |
|---|---|---|
| **Officers Cruizing Station Vessel.** | G D N | Shall I put the first turn Officers on board of Cruizing Station Vessel? |
| | G D P | Take all Officers from Cruizing Station Vessel. |
| | G D Q | Shall I take all Officers from Cruizing Station Vessel? |
| | G D R | Put all the Officers on board of Cruizing Station Vessel. |
| | G D S | Take Officers from *Vessel indicated* and put them on board of the Cruizing Station Vessel. |
| | G D T | Take Officers from *Vessel indicated* and place two-thirds with the first turns on board of Cruizing Station Vessel. |
| | G D V | Put two-thirds Officers with the first turns on board of Cruizing Station Vessel, remainder on Buoy Station Vessel. |
| | G D W | Put two-thirds Officers with the first turns on board of Cruizing Station Vessel, send me the remainder. |

# PART V.

## SENTENCES.

### No Distinguishing Flag.

| Leading Words. | Letters. | O |
|---|---|---|
| Officers Distribute. | C F B | Distribute the Officers equally on board of each Vessel according to grade and turn. |
| | C F C | Distribute the Officers as follows—two-thirds of the first turns to Cruizer, remainder equally divided between intermediate and Buoy Station Vessel which will take the last turns. |
| | C F D | Distribute the Officers as follows—two-thirds to Cruizer of the first turns, remainder to Buoy Station Vessel. |
| | C F H | I shall send you orders regarding the distribution of Officers. |
| | C F J | How shall I distribute the Officers? |
| | C F K | I will send written instructions regarding the distribution of Officers. |
| | C F L | Distribute Officers to each Vessel according to orders. |
| | C F M | Come to me for orders regarding the distribution of Officers. |

# PART V.

## SENTENCES.

### No Distinguishing Flag.

| Leading Words. | Letters. | O |
|---|---|---|
| Officers Eastern Channel Light Ship. | G F N | Are there any Officers on board of Eastern Channel Light Ship ? |
| | G F P | There are Officers on board of Eastern Channel Light Ship. |
| | G F Q | There are no Officers on board of Eastern Channel Light Ship. |
| | G F R | Enquire if there are any Officers on board of Eastern Channel Light Ship. |
| | G F S | Eastern Channel Light Ship has Officers on board. |
| | G F T | Eastern Channel Light Ship has no Officers on board. |
| Officers Enquire. | G F V | Enquire if Officer *No. indicated* is on his way down. |
| | G F W | Enquire of Officers if *Vessel indicated* is on her way down. |

# PART V.

## SENTENCES.

### No Distinguishing Flag.

| Leading Words. | Letters. | ·O |
|---|---|---|
| Officers enquire. | G H B | Enquire of Officers when *Vessel indicated* is expected in. |
| | G H C | Enquire of Officers if there is any news of *Vessel or Person indicated*. |
| | G H D | Enquire of Officer latest out how many Vessels he has passed between the Station and Saugor coming down. |
| | G H F | Enquire of Officer latest out how many Vessels he has passed between the Station and Mud Point coming down. |
| | G H J | Enquire of Officer latest out how many Vessels he has passed between the Station and Diamond Harbour coming down. |
| | G H K | Enquire of Officer latest out how many Vessels he has passed between the Station and Calcutta coming down. |
| | G H L | Enquire of Officer latest out if he knows of any Officers coming down as passengers in tugs, ships or steamers. |
| | G H M | Officer *indicated* passed number of Vessels *indicated* between the Station and Saugor coming down. |

# PART V.

## SENTENCES.

### No Distinguishing Flag.

| Leading Words. | Letters. | O |
|---|---|---|
| Officers enquire. | G H N | Officer *indicated* passed number of Vessels *indicated* between the Station and Mud Point coming down. |
| | G H P | Officer *indicated* passed number of Vessels *indicated* between the Station and Diamond Harbour coming down. |
| | G H Q | Officer *indicated* passed number of Vessels *indicated* between the Station and Calcutta coming down. |
| | G H R | Officer *indicated* does not know the number of Vessels coming down between the different Stations. |
| | G H S | Officer *indicated* knows that there are Officers coming down to the Station as passengers. |
| | G H T | Officer *indicated* does not know of any Officers coming down to the Station as passengers. |
| Officers expected. | G H V | What Officers are expected out in ships ? |
| | G H W | There are *No. indicated* expected out. |

# PART V.

## SENTENCES.

### No Distinguishing Flag.

| Leading Words. | Letters. | O |
|---|---|---|
| **Officers expected.** | G J B | There are no Officers expected out. |
| | G J C | *Vessel indicated* hourly expected with Officers. |
| | G J D | *Vessel indicated* hourly expected for Officers. |
| | G J F | *Vessel indicated* expected to-day with Officers. |
| | G.J H | *Vessel indicated* expected to-night with Officers. |
| | G J K | *Vessel indicated* expected to-morrow with Officers. |
| | G J L | When may we expect Officers? |
| | G J M | I cannot tell when we may expect Officers. |
| **Officers Grade.** | G J N | Of what grade is the Officer of the first turn? |
| | G J P | Of what grade is the Officer of the last turn? |
| | G J Q | Of what grade is the Officer that has been carried off? |
| | G J R | Of what grade is the Officer that wishes to return? |
| | G J S | Of what grade is the Officer that holds an application? |
| | G J T | Of what grade is the Officer that holds a return order? |
| | G J V | Have you an Officer of the grade of Branch or Brevet Branch on board? |
| | G J W | I have an Officer of the grade of Branch on board. |

# PART V.

## SENTENCES.

### No Distinguishing Flag.

| Leading Words. | Letters. | O |
|---|---|---|
| Officers. | G K B | I have an Officer of the grade of Brevet Branch on board. |
| | G K C | I have not an Officer of the grade of Branch or Brevet Branch on board. |
| | G K D | I have no Officer of the grade of Branch or Master on board. |
| Officers Intermediate Vessel. | G K F | What Officers are there on board of Intermediate Vessel? |
| | G K H | What Officers did you leave on board of Intermediate Vessel? |
| | G K J | Put Officers *as indicated* on board of Intermediate Vessel. |
| | G K L | Take Officers *as indicated* from Intermediate Vessel. |
| | G K M | Divide the Officers between Intermediate Vessel and yourself. |
| | G K N | Direct Intermediate Vessel to put Officers *as indicated* on board of you. |
| | G K P | Take all the Officers from Intermediate Vessel. |
| Officers Junior. | G K Q | Have you any of my Junior Officers on board? |
| | G K R | I have some of your Junior Officers on board. |
| | G K S | Send on board all my Junior Officers. |
| | G K T | Do not put out any of my Junior Officers. |
| | G K V | Can you send me a Junior Officer to do Mate's duty? |
| | G K W | I can send you a Junior Officer to do Mate's duty. |

# PART V.

## SENTENCES.

### No Distinguishing Flag.

| Leading Words. | Letters. | O |
|---|---|---|
| **Officers Junior.** | **G L B** | I cannot send you a Junior Officer to do Mate's duty. |
| **Officers Keep.** | **G L C** | Keep the Senior Officer of the turn for English Mail Steamer. |
| | **G L D** | Keep Officers *as indicated* for *Vessel indicated.* |
| | **G L F** | Shall I keep Senior Officer for English Mail Steamer ? |
| | **G L H** | Shall I keep Senior Officer for *Vessel indicated ?* |
| | **G L J** | I will send written instructions regarding the keeping of an Officer for *Vessel or purpose indicated.* |
| | **G L K** | Keep only Officers *No. indicated* at the Station till further orders. |
| | **G L M** | Keep *No. and grade indicated* for troop ships till further orders. |

# PART V.

## SENTENCES.

### No Distinguishing Flag.

| Leading Words. | Letters. | O |
|---|---|---|
| Officers Leave. | G L N | *Officer indicated* has leave—can he return to Town ? |
| | G L P | Leave Officers *as indicated* on board of *Vessel indicated.* |
| | G L Q | Leave Officers *as indicated* on board of Buoy Station Vessel. |
| | G L R | Leave Officers *as indicated* on board of Intermediate Station Vessel. |
| | G L S | Leave Officers *as indicated* on board of Cruizing Station Vessel. |
| | G L T | Leave Officer *as indicated* on board of Ridge Light to do duty as Commander. |
| | G L V | Leave Officer *as indicated* on board of Ridge Light to do duty as Chief Officer. |
| | G L W | Leave Officer *as indicated* on board of Eastern Channel Light to do duty as Commander. |

# PART V.

## SENTENCES.

### No Distinguishing Flag.

| Leading Words. | Letters. | O |
|---|---|---|
| **Officers Leave.** | C M B | Leave Officer *as indicated* on board of Eastern Channel Light to do duty as Chief Officer. |
| | C M C | Leave Officer *as indicated* on board of Lower Gasper Light to do duty as Commander. |
| | C M D | Leave Officer *as indicated* on board of Lower Gasper Light to do duty as Chief Officer. |
| | C M F | Leave Officer *as indicated* on board of Upper Gasper Light to do duty as Commander. |
| | C M H | Leave Officer *as indicated* on board of Upper Gasper Light to do duty as Chief Officer. |
| | C M J | Leave Officer *as indicated* on board of Ridge Light to do duty as Pilot. |
| | C M K | Leave Officer *as indicated* on board of Eastern Channel Light to do duty as Pilot. |
| | C M L | Leave Officer *as indicated* on board of Lower Gasper Light to do duty as Pilot. |

## SENTENCES.

### No Distinguishing Flag.

| Leading Words. | Letters. | O |
|---|---|---|
| **Officers Leave.** | **C M N** | Leave Officer *as indicated* on board of Upper Gasper Light to do duty as Pilot. |
| | **C M P** | Leave all the Officers on board of Buoy Station Vessel. |
| | **C M Q** | Leave all the Officers on board of Intermediate Station Vessel. |
| | **C M R** | Leave all the Officers on board of Cruizing Station Vessel. |
| **Officers Name.** | **C M S** | Name the Senior Officer you have on board. |
| | **C M T** | Name the Junior Officer you have on board. |
| | **C M V** | Signalize the name of the first turn Branch Pilot on board. |
| | **C M W** | Signalize the name of the last turn Branch Pilot on board. |

# PART V.

## SENTENCES.

### No Distinguishing Flag.

| Leading Words. | Letters. | O |
|---|---|---|
| **Officers Name.** | G N B | Signalize the name of the first turn Brevet Branch you have on board. |
| | G N C | Signalize the name of the last turn Brevet Branch you have on board. |
| | G N D | Signalize the name of the first turn Master on board. |
| | G N F | Signalize the name of the last turn Master on board. |
| | G N H | Signalize the name of the first turn Mate on board. |
| | G N J | Signalize the name of the last turn Mate on board. |
| | G N K | Signalize the name of the first turn Officer on board. |
| | G N L | Signalize the names of all the Officers on board. |
| **Officers Number.** | G N M | What number of Officers have you on board ? |
| | G N P | I have *No. indicated* of Officers on board. |
| | G N Q | Ascertain number of Officers on board of Buoy Station Vessel. |
| | G N R | Ascertain number of Officers on board of Intermediate Station Vessel. |
| | G N S | Ascertain number of Officers on board of Cruizing Station Vessel. |
| **Officers Orders.** | G N T | Have you any orders regarding the Officers ? |
| | G N V | I have written orders regarding the Officers. |
| | G N W | I have verbal orders regarding the Officers. |

# PART V.
##### —
## SENTENCES.
### No Distinguishing Flag.

| Leading Words. | Letters. | O |
|---|---|---|
| **Officers Orders.** | G P B | I have no orders regarding the Officers. |
| | G P C | Go to Senior Officer for orders regarding the Officers. |
| | G P D | Go to *Vessel indicated* for orders regarding the Officers. |
| | G P F | Shall I act up to orders received regarding Officers ? |
| | G P H | Shall I act up to orders received regarding Officer *as indicated* ? |
| **Officers Place.** | G P J | Place Officer *as indicated* in Command. |
| | G P K | Place Senior Officer in Command of *Vessel indicated.* |
| | G P L | Place Officer *as indicated* on board of *Vessel indicated.* |
| | G P M | Place Officer *as indicated* in Command of *Vessel indicated.* |
| **Officers Proceed.** | G P N | Proceed to Saugor with Officers. |
| | G P Q | Proceed to Kedgree with Officers. |
| | G P R | Proceed to Diamond Harbour with Officers. |
| | G P S | Proceed to Calcutta with Officers. |
| | G P T | Proceed to *place indicated* with Officer or Officers *as indicated.* |
| | G P V | Proceed to Eastern Channel for Officers. |
| | G P W | Proceed to Kedgree for Officers. |

| Leading Words. | Letters. | O |
|---|---|---|
| Officers Proceed. | G Q B | Proceed to Diamond Harbour for Officers. |
| | G Q C | Proceed to Calcutta for Officers. |
| | G Q D | Proceed to Ridge Light Station with Officers. |
| | G Q F | Proceed to Eastern Channel Light Station with Officers. |
| | G Q H | When you have put out your last Officer, proceed to *Vessel or place indicated* for more. |
| | G Q J | Proceed to the Cruizing Station with Officers. |
| | G Q K | Proceed to the Cruizing Station for Officers. |
| | G Q L | For a supply of Officers you must proceed to *Vessel or place indicated.* |

# PART V.

## SENTENCES.

### No Distinguishing Flag.

| Leading Words. | Letters. | O |
|---|---|---|
| Officers Proceed. | G Q M | Proceed into Port with the Officers who have been longest out to be sent to Town. |
| | G Q N | Proceed into Port with the Officers you have on board to be sent to Town. |
| | G Q P | Before you proceed into Port leave *No. and grade indicated* at Station and take the rest to Town. |
| Officers Put. | G Q R | Put Officers according to grade and turn on board of Vessel in want of Pilots. |
| | G Q S | Put Officers on board of Buoy Station Vessel. |
| | G Q T | Put Officers on board of Intermediate Station Vessel. |
| | G Q V | Put Officers on board of Cruizing Station Vessel. |
| | G Q W | Put Officers on board of *Vessel indicated.* |

## SENTENCES.

### No Distinguishing Flag.

| LEADING WORDS. | LETTERS. | O |
|---|---|---|
| **Officers Report.** | **G R B** | Will you report to Senior Officer my Commander is sick and requires to be relieved? |
| | **G R C** | Will you report to Senior Officer my Chief Officer is sick and requires to be relieved? |
| | **G R D** | Will you report to Senior Officer my Second Officer is sick and requires to be relieved? |
| | **G R F** | Report to Senior Officer at Cruizing Station *as indicated*. |
| | **G R H** | I will report to Senior Officer at Cruizing Station *as indicated*. |
| | **G R J** | Report to Master Attendant by Electric Telegraph at Saugor the want of Officers at the Cruizing Station. |
| | **G R K** | Report to Master Attendant by Electric Telegraph at Saugor that there are no Officers at the Cruizing Station. |
| | **G R L** | Report to Master Attendant by Electric Telegraph at Saugor ships are waiting for Pilots at Cruizing Stations. |

# PART V.

## SENTENCES.

### No Distinguishing Flag.

| Leading Words. | Letters. | O |
|---|---|---|
| **Officers Report.** | G R M | Report to Master Attendant by Electric Telegraph at Saugor *as indicated.* |
| **Officers Require.** | G R N | Officers are required in Calcutta. |
| | G R P | Officers are required at Cruizing Station. |
| **Officers Returning.** | G R Q | All Officers to return from *Vessel indicated.* |
| | G R S | All Officers returning pay their own passage. |
| | G R T | All Officers returning pay the usual rate of mess. |
| | G R V | All Officers to return on duty. |
| | G R W | Allow Officer *indicated* to return. |

# PART V.

## SENTENCES.

### No Distinguishing Flag.

| Leading Words. | Letters. | O |
|---|---|---|
| **Officers Return-ing.** | G S B | Can Officer *indicated* be allowed to return ? |
| | G S C | Allow Officer *indicated* to return at his own expense. |
| | G S D | Officer *indicated* can return. |
| | G S F | Officer *indicated* cannot return. |
| | G S H | Officer *indicated* cannot return—services cannot be spared. |
| | G S J | Officer *indicated* wishes to return. |
| | G S K | Officer *indicated* does not wish to return. |
| | G S L | Officer or Officers *indicated* holds a return order unconditional,—can he make use of it ? |

*Officer indicated can give no reason for wishing to return*

## SENTENCES.

### No Distinguishing Flag.

| Leading Words. | Letters. | O |
|---|---|---|
| **Officers Return Order.** | G S M | Officer or Officers *indicated* holds a return order conditional,—can he make use of it? |
| | G S N | Officer with unconditional return order can go to Town as passenger by first opportunity. |
| | G S P | Officer with conditional return order can go to Town as passenger by first opportunity. |
| | G S Q | Officer with unconditional return order place as Pilot in the first ship of his class. |
| | G S R | Officer with conditional return order place as Pilot in the first ship of his class. |
| | G S T | Officer with unconditional return order place as Pilot in the first ship in his regular turn. |
| | G S V | Officer with conditional return order place as Pilot in the first ship in his regular turn. |
| | G S W | All Officers whether holding conditional or unconditional return orders can make use of them. |

# PART V.

—

## SENTENCES.

### No Distinguishing Flag.

| Leading Words. | Letters. | O |
|---|---|---|
| Officers Return Order. | G T B | Allow no Officer whether holding a conditional or unconditional return order to make use of them. |
| Officers Return Orders. | G T C | Await further instructions regarding return orders. |
| | G T D | I will send written instructions regarding return orders. |
| | G T F | When return orders are received, if within signal distance, lose no time in communicating the same to me. |
| Officers Ridge Light. | G T H | Are there any Officers on board of Ridge Light? |
| | G T J | There are Officers on board of Ridge Light. |
| | G T K | Enquire if there are any Officers on board of Ridge Light. |
| | G T L | Shall I enquire if there are any Officers on board of Ridge Light? |
| | G T M | Ridge Light has Officers on board. |
| | G T N | Ridge Light has no Officers on board. |
| Officers Second. | G T P | Second Officer. |
| | G T Q | Have you my Second Officer on board? |
| | G T R | I have your Second Officer on board. |
| | G T S | I have not your Second Officer on board. |
| | G T V | Send your Second Officer on board. |
| | G T W | Do you know if my Second Officer is on his way down? |

# PART V.

## SENTENCES.

### No Distinguishing Flag.

| Leading Words. | Letters. | O |
|---|---|---|
| **Officers Second.** | G V B | I have been compelled to put my Second Officer on board of a Vessel. |
| | G V C | I have been compelled to send my Second Officer to Town. |
| | G V D | I am without a Second Officer. |
| | G V F | My Second Officer is ill. |
| | G V H | My Second Officer is drowned. |
| | G V J | My Second Officer is dead. |
| | G V K | My Second Officer is too ill to remain on board any longer. |
| | G V L | My Second Officer is dangerously ill. |
| | G V M | Your Second Officer is on his way down. |
| | G V N | You may expect your Second Officer in *Vessel indicated.* |
| | G V P | I will relieve your Second Officer. |
| | G V Q | I have no news of your Second Officer. |
| | G V R | Can you relieve my Second Officer ? |
| | G V S | I cannot relieve your Second Officer. |
| **Officers Send.** | G V T | Shall I send you the Officers ? |
| | G V W | Send me all the Officers. |

# PART V.

—

## SENTENCES.

### No Distinguishing Flag.

| Leading Words. | Letters. | O |
|---|---|---|
| **Officers Send.** | G W B | Send me Officers *as indicated*. |
| | G W C | Send me *as indicated*. |
| | G W D | Send me No. and grade of first turn. |
| | G W F | Send me No. and grade of last turn. |
| | G W H | Send Officer *indicated* to Town first opportunity as Passenger. |
| | G W J | Send Officer *indicated* to Town first opportunity as Pilot. |
| | G W K | Send me Officers at daylight to-morrow. |
| | G W L | Send me Officers now. |
| | G W M | Send me Officers after breakfast. |
| | G W N | Send me Officers after dinner. |
| | G W P | Send me Officers when I have supplied the ships close to with Pilots. |
| | G W Q | Send me Officers when directed. |
| | G W R | Send for the Officers. |
| | G W S | Send Officers *indicated* on board of *Vessel indicated*. |
| | G W T | Send for the Officers at daylight to-morrow. |
| | G W V | Send for the Officers after breakfast. |

# PART V.

## SENTENCES.

### No Distinguishing Flag.

| Leading Words. | Letters. | O |
|---|---|---|
| Officers Send. | H B C | Send for the Officers after dinner. |
| | H B D | I will send for the Officers. |
| | H B F | I will send for the Officers at daylight to-morrow. |
| | H B G | I will send for the Officers after breakfast. |
| | H B J | I will send for the Officers after dinner. |
| | H B K | I will send for the Officers when I have taken Pilots out of Vessels close to. |
| | H B L | I will send the Officers. |
| | H B M | I will send the Officers at daylight to-morrow. |
| | H B N | I will send the Officers now. |
| | H B P | I will send the Officers after breakfast. |
| | H B Q | I will send the Officers after dinner. |
| | H B R | I will send all the Officers. |
| | H B S | Shall I send for the Officers ? |
| | H B T | Do not send me any more Officers. |
| | H B V | Will you send the Officers ? |
| | H B W | Will you send all the Officers ? |

| LEADING WORDS. | LETTERS. | O |
|---|---|---|
| Officers Send. | H C B | Will you send for the Officers ? |
| | H C D | When shall I send the Officers ? |
| | H C F | When shall I send for the Officers ? |
| | H C G | Send all the Officers on board *Vessel indicated.* |
| | H C J | Send number and grade *indicated* on board of *Vessel indicated.* |
| | H C K | Send number and grade *indicated* of first turn on board of *Vessel indicated.* |
| | H C L | Send number and grade *indicated* of last turn on board of *Vessel indicated.* |
| | H C M | Send number and grade *indicated* of first turn to Town paying their own passage. |
| | H C N | Send number and grade *indicated* of first turn to Town on duty. |
| | H C P | Send number and grade *indicated* of last turn to Town paying their own passage. |
| | H C Q | Send number and grade *indicated* of last turn to Town on duty. |
| Officers Senior. | H C R | Senior Officer. |
| | H C S | Who is the Senior Officer ? |
| | H C T | Where is the Senior Officer ? |
| | H C V | The Senior Officer is *as indicated.* |
| | H C W | The Senior Officer required for *purpose indicated.* |

*Send Officers at High Water*

*"  "   "   "  Low*

*"  for  "   "  High Water*

*"   "   "   "  Low*

# PART V.

## SENTENCES.

### No Distinguishing Flag.

| LEADING WORDS. | LETTERS. | O |
|---|---|---|
| **Officers Senior.** | H D B | A Senior Officer required for *purpose indicated*. |
| | H D C | The Senior Officer required for Admiral Ship—retain him. |
| | H D F | The Senior Officer required for Commodore Ship—retain him. |
| | H D G | The Senior Officer required for Line of Battle Ship—retain him. |
| | H D J | The Senior Officer required for First Class Frigates—retain him. |
| | H D K | The Senior Officer required for English Mail Steamer—retain him. |
| | H D L | A Senior Officer required for English Mail Steamer—retain him. |
| | H D M | The Senior Officer is required for *purpose indicated*—retain him. |
| | H D N | Shall I keep the Senior Officer for English Mail Steamer ? |
| | H D P | Shall I keep a Senior Officer for English Mail Steamer ? |
| | H D Q | Shall I keep the Senior Officer for Admiral's Ship ? |
| | H D R | Shall I keep the Senior Officer for Commodore's Ship ? |
| | H D S | Shall I keep the Senior Officer for Line of Battle Ship ? |
| | H D T | Shall I keep the Senior Officer for First Class Frigate ? |
| **Officers Sick.** | H D V | A sick Officer. |
| | H D W | Who is the sick Officer ? |

# PART V.

## SENTENCES.

### No Distinguishing Flag.

| Leading Words. | Letters. | O |
|---|---|---|
| **Officers Sick.** | H F B | Officer is sick and cannot take charge of a Ship. |
| | H F C | Is the Officer left on board sick fit for duty ? |
| | H F D | Is the Officer left on board sick any better ? |
| | H F G | Is the Officer left on board sick any worse ? |
| | H F J | Sick Officer is better. |
| | H F K | Sick Officer is worse. |
| | H F L | Sick Officer is fit for duty. |
| | H F M | Sick Officer is dead. |
| | H F N | Sick Officer is gone to Calcutta. |
| | H F P | I will send the Officer left on board sick now. |
| | H F Q | I will send the Officer left on board sick to-morrow. |
| | H F R | I will send the Officer left on board sick as soon as able. |
| | H F S | Officer *No. and grade* is taken sick. |
| **Officers Take.** | H F T | How many Officers shall I take ? |
| | H F V | Take no Officers. |
| | H F W | Take all the Officers. |

# PART V.

## SENTENCES.

### No Distinguishing Flag.

| Leading Words. | Letters. | O |
|---|---|---|
| **Officers Take.** | **H C B** | Take Officers of first turn *as indicated*. |
| | **H C C** | Take Officers of last turn *as indicated*. |
| | **H C D** | Shall I take the Officers? |
| | **H C F** | Take Officers from *Vessel indicated*. |
| **Officers Traps.** | **H C J** | Officer *indicated* has left his traps behind. |
| | **H C K** | Part of Officer's *indicated* traps have been left behind. |
| | **H C L** | Send the Officer without his traps which can follow. |
| **Officers Turns.** | **H C M** | Who is the Officer of the turn? |
| | **H C N** | What is the grade of the Officer of the turn? |
| | **H C P** | What Vessel has the Officer of the turn? |
| | **H C Q** | I have the Officer of the turn. |
| | **H C R** | The Officer of the turn is a Branch Pilot. |
| | **H C S** | The Officer of the turn is a Brevet Branch Pilot. |
| | **H C T** | The Officer of the turn is a Senior Master. |
| | **H C V** | The Officer of the turn is a Junior Master. |
| | **H C W** | The Officer of the turn is a Mate. |

*Officer (indicated) has turn (indicated)*
*What turn has officer (indicated)*
*Officer indicated has last turn*

## SENTENCES.

### No Distinguishing Flag.

| Leading Words. | Letters. | O |
|---|---|---|
| **Officers Turn.** | H J B | Will the Officer of the turn take the Vessel in sight ? |
| | H J C | The Officer of the turn will take the Vessel in sight. |
| | H J D | The Officer of the turn gives up the Vessel in sight. |
| | H J F | Officer of turn can give up a Vessel to Officer of same grade. |
| | H J G | All Officers to take their respective turns. |
| | H J K | Officers according to their turns place on board of Vessels wanting Pilots. |
| | H J L | Officer according to his turn place on board of Vessel wanting Pilots. |
| | H J M | You have the Officer of the turn. |
| | H J N | You have not the Officer of the turn. |
| **Officers between Saugor and Station.** | H J P | How many Officers did you leave between the Saugor and Eastern Channel Lights outward bound ? |
| **Oil.** | H J Q | I am in want of paint oil. |
| | H J R | I am in want of burning oil. |
| | H J S | The Light Station oil is nearly expended. |
| | H J T | I have oil for days *indicated*. |
| | H J V | Can you supply me with paint oil ? |
| | H J W | Can you supply me with burning oil ? |

# PART V.

## SENTENCES.

### No Distinguishing Flag.

| Leading Words. | Letters. | O |
|---|---|---|
| Oil. | H K B | I cannot show the lights for the want of oil. |
| | H K C | The burning oil is so bad that it cannot be used. |
| | H K D | The burning oil is so bad that lights will not burn brightly. |
| One. | H K F | As *indicated* in one. |
| Open. | H K G | As *indicated* open to the North. |
| | H K J | As *indicated* open to the South. |
| | H K L | As *indicated* open to the East. |
| | H K M | As *indicated* open to the West. |
| Opportunity. | H K N | When an opportunity offers. |
| | H K P | When will an opportunity offer? |
| | H K Q | An opportunity will offer on *date indicated.* |
| | H K R | Embrace the present opportunity. |
| | H K S | The present is a good opportunity. |
| | H K T | It is a good opportunity. |
| Orders. | H K V | Have you received any order by Electric Telegraph for me? |
| | H K W | Have you any orders for me? |

*On*
*" the*
*one*

# PART V.

## SENTENCES.

### No Distinguishing Flag.

| Leading Words. | Letters. | O |
|---|---|---|
| Orders. | **H L B** | I have orders for you. |
| | **H L C** | I have no orders for you. |
| | **H L D** | Act according to orders. |
| | **H L F** | I will send for orders. |
| | **H L G** | I have received orders to *as indicated*. |
| | **H L J** | *Person indicated* has received orders *as indicated*. |
| | **H L K** | *State) officer (indicated) holds an application or has leave to return.* |
| | **H L M** | *Officer (indicated) can give no reason for returning.* |

# PART V.

## SENTENCES.

### No Distinguishing Flag.

| Leading Words. | Letters. | P |
|---|---|---|
| Parted. | H L N | I have parted. |
| | H L P | *Vessel indicated* has parted. |
| Passenger. | H L Q | A passenger lady. |
| | H L R | A passenger gentleman. |
| | H L S | A passenger invalid. |
| | H L T | There are passengers on board *Vessels indicated* for you. |
| | H L V | There are passengers coming down for you. |
| Permission. | H L W | You have my permission. |

*Obtain permission —*

# PART V.

## SENTENCES.

### No Distinguishing Flag.

| Leading Words. | Letters. | P |
|---|---|---|
| **Permission.** | H M B | You have not my permission. |
| | H M C | Have I your permission? |
| | H M D | Has given permission. |
| | H M F | Has not given permission. |
| **Pilot on Board.** | H M G | Put a Pilot on board of the strangers. |
| | H M J | Shall I put a Pilot on board of the strangers? |
| | H M K | I will put a Pilot on board of the strangers. |
| | H M L | I have put a Pilot on board of the strangers. |
| | H M N | I have not put a Pilot on board of the strangers. |
| *Pilots Branch* | H M P | I have a Branch Pilot on board. |
| | H M Q | I have a Brevet Branch Pilot on board. |
| | H M R | I have a Senior Master Pilot on board. |
| | H M S | I have a Junior Master Pilot on board. |
| | H M T | I have a Senior Mate Pilot on board. |
| | H M V | I have a Junior Mate Pilot on board. |
| | H M W | I have a Leadsman on board. |
| | | *" " no Branch Pilot on board* |
| | | *" " " B " " "* |
| | | *Have you a Branch Pilot on boar* |
| | | *" " " B " " "* |

# PART V.

## SENTENCES.

### No Distinguishing Flag.

| Leading Words. | Letters. | P |
|---|---|---|
| **Pilot on Board.** | H N B | Put a Branch Pilot on board of the strangers. |
| | H N C | Put a Brevet Branch Pilot on board of the strangers. |
| | H N D | Put a Master Senior Pilot on board of the strangers. |
| | H N F | Put a Master Junior Pilot on board of the strangers. |
| | H N G | Put a Mate Senior Pilot on board of the strangers. |
| | H N J | Put a Mate Junior Pilot on board of the strangers. |
| | H N K | There is no Pilot on board of the strangers. |
| | H N L | Who shall I put as Pilot on board of Ship? |
| | H N M | Put *grade indicated* as Pilot on board of Ship. |
| | H N P | Put yourself on board of Ship as Pilot. |
| | H N Q | Put Pilots on board of Ship without any delay. |
| **Pilot carried off.** | H N R | *Vessel indicated* has carried off her Pilot. |
| | H N S | English Mail Steamer has carried off her Pilot. |
| | H N T | French Mail Steamer has carried off her Pilot. |
| | H N V | China Mail Steamer has carried off her Pilot. |
| | H N W | East Coast Mail Steamer has carried off her Pilot. |

# PART V.

## SENTENCES.

### No Distinguishing Flag.

| Leading Words. | Letters. | P |
|---|---|---|
| Pilot carried off. | H P B | West Coast Mail Steamer has carried off her Pilot. |
| Pilot Grade. | H P C | Pilot Branch. |
| | H P D | Pilot Brevet Branch. |
| | H P F | Pilot Senior Master. |
| | H P G | Pilot Junior Master. |
| | H P J | Pilot Senior Mate. |
| | H P K | Pilot Junior Mate. |
| | H P L | Pilot Leadsman. |
| Pilot Keep. | H P M | Keep a Pilot for *purpose indicated*. |
| | H P N | Keep Branch Pilot of the turn for English Mail. |
| | H P Q | Keep Brevet Branch Pilot of the turn for English Mail. |
| | H P R | Keep Senior Master Pilot of the turn for English Mail. |
| | H P S | Keep *No. and grade indicated* as Pilots for H. M.'s Ships of War. |
| | H P T | Keep *No. and grade indicated* as Pilots for H. M.'s Transports. |
| | H P V | Keep *No. and grade indicated* as Pilots for large Vessels. |
| Pilot Obtain. | H P W | Accompany stranger or strangers to *place indicated*, and obtain Pilots for them. |
| *Pilot Master* | | *Have you a Master Pilot on board* / *I have not " " " "* |
| *Pilot Mate* | | *Have you a Mate Pilot on board* / *I have " " " "* |

*" " not " " " "*

# PART V.

## SENTENCES.

### No Distinguishing Flag.

| Leading Words. | Letters. | P |
|---|---|---|
| Pilot Obtain. | H Q B | Endeavour to obtain a Pilot for me. |
| Pilot Question. | H Q C | Who is her Pilot ? |
| | H Q D | Who is your Pilot ? |
| | H Q F | Who is the Pilot of *Vessel indicated ?* |
| | H Q G | Do not know who is the Pilot of *Vessel indicated.* |
| Pilot Relieve. | H Q J | Relieve Pilot from *Vessel indicated.* |
| | H Q K | Pilot of *Vessel indicated* wishes to be relieved. |
| | H Q L | Pilot of *Vessel indicated* cannot be relieved. |
| | H Q M | No one to relieve Pilot from *Vessel indicated.* |
| | H Q N | Shall I relieve Pilot from *Vessel indicated ?* |
| Pilots Send. | H Q P | Send me all the Branch Pilots. |
| | H Q R | Send me all the Brevet Branch Pilots. |
| | H Q S | Send me all the Senior Master Pilots. |
| | H Q T | Send me all the Junior Master Pilots. |
| | H Q V | Send me all the Senior Mate Pilots. |
| | H Q W | Send me all the Junior Mate Pilots. |

# PART V.

## SENTENCES.

### No Distinguishing Flag.

| Leading Words. | Letters. | P |
|---|---|---|
| Pilot Send. | H R B | Send me all the Leadsmen. |
| | H R C | Send a Pilot to Ship in a Tug if one communicates. |
| | H R D | Send Pilots to the different Ships in Tugs if possible. |
| | H R F | Will you assist in sending Pilots to Ships ? |
| Pilots Supply. | H R G | Supply Ships in sight with Pilots. |
| | H R J | Have you supplied Ships in sight with Pilots ? |
| | H R K | I have supplied Ships in sight with Pilots. |
| | H R L | I have not supplied Ships in sight with Pilots. |
| | H R M | I am going to supply Ships in sight with Pilots. |
| | H R N | Have you supplied Ships during the night with Pilots ? |
| | H R P | I have supplied Ships during the night with Pilots. |
| | H R Q | Supply Vessels in distress first with Pilots. |
| | H R S | Supply H. M.'s Transport Steamers first with Pilots. |
| | H R T | Supply H. M.'s Transport Ships first with Pilots. |
| | H R V | Supply Troop Ships first with Pilots. |
| | H R W | Supply Emigrant Ships first with Pilots |

# PART V.

## SENTENCES.

### No Distinguishing Flag.

| LEADING WORDS. | LETTERS. | P |
|---|---|---|
| **Pilots Supply.** | **H S B** | Supply Convict Ships first with Pilots. |
| | **H S C** | Supply Horse Ships first with Pilots. |
| | **H S D** | Supply Elephant Ships first with Pilots. |
| | **H S F** | Supply Bullock Ships first with Pilots. |
| | **H S G** | Supply Mule Ships first with Pilots. |
| | **H S J** | Supply Camel Ships first with Pilots. |
| | **H S K** | Supply Pilgrims' Ships first with Pilots. |
| | **H S L** | I have supplied *Vessel indicated* with a Pilot. |
| | **H S M** | I have not supplied *Vessel indicated* with a Pilot. |
| | **H S N** | Have you supplied *Vessel indicated* with a Pilot? |
| **Pilots Take out.** | **H S P** | Take Pilots out of Vessels in sight. |
| | **H S Q** | Take Pilots out of Vessels near. |
| | **H S R** | Assist me in taking Pilots out of Vessels in sight. |
| | **H S T** | Assist me in taking Pilots out of Vessels near. |
| | **H S V** | I have taken out *person indicated*. |
| | **H S W** | I will take you out immediately. |

# PART V.

## SENTENCES.

### No Distinguishing Flag.

| Leading Words. | Letters. | P |
|---|---|---|
| Pilots Taken Out. | H T B | Have you taken out *person indicated ?* |
| | H T C | I have taken out *person indicated.* |
| | H T D | I have not taken out *person indicated.* |
| | H T F | Have you taken the Pilots out of the Vessels in sight ? |
| | H T G | Have you taken the Pilots out of the Vessels near ? |
| | H T J | Will you take the Pilots out of the Vessels in sight ? |
| | H T K | Will you take the Pilots out of the Vessels near ? |
| | H T L | I have taken the Pilots out of the Vessels in sight. |
| | H T M | I have taken the Pilots out of the Vessels near. |
| | H T N | I have not taken the Pilots out of the Vessels.—*Name or bearing as indicated.* |
| | H T P | I will take the Pilots out of the Vessels in sight. |
| | H T Q | I will take the Pilots out of the Vessels near. |
| | H T R | Shall I take the Pilots out of the Vessels in sight ? |
| | H T S | Shall I take the Pilots out of the Vessels near ? |
| | H T V | Have you taken any Pilots out during the night ? |
| | H T W | I have taken Pilots out during the night. |

# PART V.

## SENTENCES.

### No Distinguishing Flag.

| Leading Words. | Letters. | P |
|---|---|---|
| **Pilots Taken Out.** | H V B | Do not take the Pilot out till high water. |
| | H V C | Take Pilots out of Ships without any delay. |
| | H V D | Will you take me out ? |
| | H V F | I will take you out at high water. |
| | H V G | I will take you out when aweigh. |
| | H V J | Follow me into smooth water and I will take you out. |
| | H V K | Circumstances prevent my taking you out. |
| | H V L | I cannot quit my station to take you out. |
| | H V M | My Crew are too fatigued to take you out. |
| | H V N | If you wish to be taken out you will have to come in your own boat. |
| | H V P | Too much sea to take you out. |
| | H V Q | Commander of Ship does not wish me to be taken out now. |
| | H V R | Commander of Ship does not wish me to be taken out now until high water. |
| | H V S | Cannot weigh my anchor to take you out. |
| **Pilots wanted.** | H V T | Pilots wanted for Vessels at *place indicated*. |
| | H V W | Pilots wanted for Vessels leaky at *place indicated*. |

# PART V.

## SENTENCES.

### No Distinguishing Flag.

| LEADING WORDS. | LETTERS. | P |
|---|---|---|
| **Wanted.** | H W B | Pilots wanted for Vessels lost rudder at *place indicated.* |
| | H W C | Pilots wanted for Vessels on shore at *place indicated.* |
| | H W D | Pilots wanted for Vessels dismasted at *place indicated.* |
| | H W F | Pilots wanted for Vessels without anchor at *place indicated.* |
| | H W G | Signalize to Vessels in want of Pilots to anchor. |
| | H W J | Signalize to Vessels in want of Pilots to go to sea till the weather changes. |
| | H W K | Signalize to Vessels in want of Pilots to keep to seaward. |
| | H W L | Can I take Pilotage charge of this Ship or Steamer ?—*Name or Private Flag to follow.* |
| **Port.** | H W M | I am bound into Port. |
| | H W N | When can I proceed into Port ? |
| | H W P | When shall I proceed into Port ? |
| | H W Q | Proceed into Port now. |
| | H W R | Proceed into Port *time indicated.* |
| | H W S | When will you proceed into Port ? |
| | H W T | I shall proceed into Port now or *at time indicated.* |
| | H W V | I am obliged to proceed into Port. |

NOTE.—This signal H. W. L. to be used on arriving at the Station on the return of any Officer after having been carried off.

# PART V.

## SENTENCES.

### No Distinguishing Flag.

| LEADING WORDS. | LETTERS. | P |
|---|---|---|
| Port. | J B C | Do not proceed into Port until you are relieved. |
| | J B D | Be in readiness to proceed into Port. |
| | J B F | Can I proceed into Port? |
| | J B G | Proceed into Port when your relief comes out. |
| | J B H | You cannot proceed into Port till your relief comes out. |
| | J B K | *Vessel indicated* has gone into Port. |
| | J B L | You can proceed into Port. |
| | J B M | You cannot proceed into Port. |
| Proceed. | J B N | Proceed to *place indicated.* |
| | J B P | Direct *Vessel indicated* to proceed to *place indicated* for *purpose indicated.* |
| | J B Q | Do not proceed to *place indicated.* |
| | J B R | Proceed to Saugor and wait for orders from Master Attendant. |
| | J B S | Proceed to Mud Point and wait for orders from Master Attendant. |
| | J B T | Proceed to Diamond Harbour and wait for orders from Master Attendant. |
| Provisions. | J B V | Are you in want of provisions? |
| | J B W | I am in want of provisions. |

# PART V.

## SENTENCES.

### No Distinguishing Flag.

| Leading Words. | Letters. | P |
|---|---|---|
| Provisions. | J C B | *Vessel indicated* is in want of provisions. |
| | J C D | Supply *Vessel indicated* with provisions. |
| | J C F | I will supply you with provisions. |
| | J C G | I am not in want of provisions. |
| | J C H | I have supplied *Vessel indicated* with provisions. |
| | J C K | Provision on board for *days indicated*. |
| | J C L | I cannot supply you with provisions. |
| | J C M | Report my want of provisions. |
| | J C N | Have no provisions to spare. |
| | J C P | I will endeavour to obtain provisions for you. |
| | J C Q | *Vessel indicated* expected with provisions. |
| | J C R | *Vessel indicated* will come with provisions. |
| Pumps. | J C S | Cannot keep her free with pumps. |
| | J C T | If unable to keep the Vessel free with pumps breach her. |
| | J C V | If unable to keep the Vessel free with pumps leave her. |
| | J C W | Send spare pumps if you have them. |

# PART V.

## SENTENCES.

### No Distinguishing Flag.

| LEADING WORDS. | LETTERS. | P |
|---|---|---|
| | J D B | |
| | J D C | |
| | J D F | |
| | J D G | |
| | J D H | |
| | J D K | |

# PART V.

## SENTENCES.

### No Distinguishing Flag.

| Leading Words. | Letters. | R |
|---|---|---|
| Rank. | J D L | To be allowed the privilege of his rank. |
| Relief. | J D M | Has my relief come out ? |
| | J D N | Your relief has come out. |
| | J D P | When am I to be relieved ? |
| | J D Q | Your relief has not come out. |
| | J D R | When will my relief be out ? |
| Relieve. | J D S | Will you relieve me for *purpose* indicated ? |
| | J D T | What Vessel relieves me ? |
| | J D V | When I am relieved. |
| | J D W | I will relieve you immediately or at time indicated. |

*Is my relief on board.*
*Has  „   „   Come down.*

# PART V.

## SENTENCES.

### No Distinguishing Flag.

| Leading Words. | Letters. | R |
|---|---|---|
| Relieve. | J F B | I will direct *Vessel indicated* to relieve you. |
| | J F C | I will direct *Officer indicated* to relieve you. |
| | J F D | Can I be relieved ? |
| | J F G | You can be relieved. |
| | J F H | You cannot be relieved. |
| | J F K | There is no person to relieve you. |
| Remain. | J F L | You must remain till you are relieved. |
| | J F M | You can remain for *purpose indicated.* |
| | J F N | You cannot remain for *purpose indicated.* |
| | J F P | Remain till further orders. |
| Report. | J F Q | Report to Master Attendant by Electric Telegragh *Vessel indicated* is totally dismasted and requires steam. |
| | J F R | Report to Master Attendant by Electric Telegraph *Vessel indicated* is waiting for steam. |
| | J F S | Report to Master Attendant by Electric Telegraph *Vessel indicated* awaits orders. |
| | J F T | Have you seen last report of Channel or Bar *indicated* ? |
| | J F V | Will you send me last report of Channel or Bar *indicated ?* |
| | J F W | You will find last report of Channel or Bar *indicated* at *place indicated.* |

## PART V.

### SENTENCES.

#### No Distinguishing Flag.

| LEADING WORDS. | LETTERS. | R |
|---|---|---|
| Report. | J G B | You will find last report of Channel or Bar *indicated*. |
| | J G C | *Person indicated* has the last report of Channel or Bar *indicated*. |
| | J G D | I have an application—can I return ? |
| | J G F | *Person indicated* has an application—can he return ? |
| | J G H | May I return in Steamer ? |
| | J G K | May I return in Ship ? |
| | J G L | May I return if my services can be spared ? |
| | J G M | I have a conditional return order—can I make use of it ? |
| | J G N | I have an unconditional return order—can I make use of it ? |
| Return. | J G P | Will you permit me to return ? |
| | J G Q | You may return in Steamer. |
| | J G R | You may return in Ship. |
| | J G S | You cannot return. |
| | J G T | *Person indicated* can return—signalize to that effect. |
| | J G V | *Person indicated* cannot return—signalize to that effect. |
| | J G W | You or *person indicated* can return. |

# PART V.

## SENTENCES.

### No Distinguishing Flag.

| Leading Words. | Letters. | R |
|---|---|---|
| Return. | J H B | You or *person indicated* cannot return. |
| Risk. | J H C | Remain at all risk. |
| | J H D | Run no risk but save life. |
| | J H F | I think it a safe risk. |
| | J H G | I think it an unsafe risk. |
| Rudder. | J H K | My Vessel's rudder is injured. |
| | J H L | My Vessel's rudder is gone. |
| | J H M | *Vessel indicated* rudder is injured. |
| | J H N | *Vessel indicated* rudder is gone. |
| | J H P | |
| | J H Q | |
| | J H R | |
| | J H S | |
| | J H T | |

# PART V.

## SENTENCES.

### No Distinguishing Flag.

| LEADING WORDS. | LETTERS. | S |
|---|---|---|
| Sails. | J H V | Sails main. |
|  | J H W | Sails main-top. |

# PART V.

## SENTENCES.

### No Distinguishing Flag.

| Leading Words. | Letters. | S |
|---|---|---|
| Sails. | J K B | Sails main-top-gallant. |
| | J K C | Sails main-royal. |
| | J K D | Sails main-stay. |
| | J K F | Sails main-boom. |
| | J K G | Sails fore. |
| | J K H | Sails fore-top. |
| | J K L | Sails fore-top-gallant. |
| | J K M | Sails fore-royal. |
| | J K N | Sails fore-topmast-stay. |
| | J K P | Sails fore-stay. |
| | J K Q | Sails jib. |
| | J K R | Sails flying jib. |
| | J K S | I am in want of Sails *as indicated*. |
| | J K T | I have split all the Sails I had bent. |
| | J K V | I have split all my Sails. |
| | J K W | Can you supply me with Sail *indicated ?* |

| Leading Words. | Letters. | S |
|---|---|---|
| Sails. | J L B | *Vessel indicated* is in want of Sails. |
| Sand. | J L C | Back of Sand *as indicated.* |
| | J L D | Head of Sand *as indicated.* |
| | J L F | Spit of Sand *as indicated.* |
| | J L G | Tail of Sand *as indicated.* |
| | J L H | Sand or Bar *indicated* has disappeared. |
| | J L K | Sand or Bar *indicated* has encroached further to *direction indicated.* |
| Sea. | J L M | At Sea. |
| | J L N | I am going to Sea. |
| | J L P | Put to Sea. |
| | J L Q | *Vessel indicated* has put to Sea. |
| | J L R | Is there much Sea in the Channel ? |
| | J L S | There is not much Sea in the Channel. |
| | J L T | There is heavy Sea in the Channel. |
| | J L V | No Sea in the Channel. |
| Seeing. | J L W | On my seeing it will be able to inform you. |

*Saturday*
*Second*

# PART V.

## SENTENCES.

### No Distinguishing Flag.

| Leading Words. | Letters. | S |
|---|---|---|
| Send. | J M B | Send at *time or date indicated.* |
| | J M C | When shall I send ? |
| | J M D | When will you send ? |
| | J M F | I will send now or on *date indicated.* |
| | J M G | I cannot send. |
| | J M H | I can send. |
| September. | J M K | September. |
| Services. | J M L | Provided his services can be spared. |
| | J M N | Do you require my services ? |
| | J M P | I do require your services. |
| | J M Q | I do require services of *Person or Vessel indicated.* |
| | J M R | Do you require services of *Person or Vessel indicated ?* |
| | J M S | I do not require services of *Person or Vessel indicated.* |
| | J M T | *Vessel or Person indicated* is at your service. |
| | J M V | I am at your service. |
| | J M W | I do not require your services. |

# PART V.

## SENTENCES.

### No Distinguishing Flag.

| Leading Words. | Letters. | S |
|---|---|---|
| Service. | J N B | Can I be of any service? |
| Set. | J N C | Is there any set? |
| | J N D | There is no set. |
| | J N F | There is strong set to *quarter indicated.* |
| | J N G | There is moderate set to *quarter indicated.* |
| Sick. | J N H | I am going in with a person dangerously sick. |
| | J N K | Proceed in with person dangerously sick. |
| | J N L | Who is the sick person? |
| | J N M | Sick person is *as indicated.* |
| | J N P | Pilot is sick and wants to be relieved. |
| Signals. | J N Q | Last Signal was a mistake. |
| | J N R | Repeat your last Signal. |
| | J N S | Repeat your Signals throughout. |
| | J N T | Do you comprehend the Signals? |
| | J N V | I do comprehend the Signals. |
| | J N W | I do not comprehend the Signals. |

# PART V.

## SENTENCES.

### No Distinguishing Flag.

| LEADING WORDS. | LETTERS. | S |
|---|---|---|
| Signals. | J P B | You are inattentive to Signals. |
| | J P C | Repeat my Signal. |
| | J P D | Repeat Signals made by *Vessels indicated*. |
| | J P F | Come within Signal distance if possible every day or date *as indicated*. |
| Sinking. | J P G | My Vessel is in a sinking state. |
| | J P H | *Vessel indicated* is in a sinking state. |
| Sound. | J P K | Will you sound for my guidance and show the water ? |
| | J P L | Will you sound to *quarter indicated* of me ? |
| | J P M | Will you sound ahead of me through the Channel ? |
| | J P N | Will you sound astern of me ? |
| | J P Q | Will you sound to the Eastward of me ? |
| | J P R | Will you sound to the Westward of me ? |
| | J P S | Will you sound to the Northward of me ? |
| | J P T | Will you sound to the Southward of me ? |
| | J P V | I am going to sound—will you join me ? |
| Soundings. | J P W | I have returned from soundings and found *No. of feet indicated* reduced. |

x Seventh
Tenth Seventeenth
Sixth

( 221 )

Sixteenth

# PART V.

---

# SENTENCES.

## No Distinguishing Flag.

| LEADING WORDS. | LETTERS. | S |
|---|---|---|
| Soundings. | J Q B | Soundings are not to be depended on. |
| | J Q C | Soundings are regular. |
| | J Q D | Soundings are irregular. |
| Station. | J Q F | Keep your Station. |
| | J Q G | Do not leave your Station. |
| | J Q H | You are not on your Station. |
| | J Q K | Are you on your Station? |
| | J Q L | I am on my Station. |
| | J Q M | I am off my Station. |
| | J Q N | Are you able to keep your Station? |
| | J Q P | I am able to keep my Station. |
| | J Q R | I am unable to keep my Station. |
| | J Q S | Take charge of the Station during my absence. |
| | J Q T | I will take charge of the Station during your absence. |
| | J Q V | Attend strictly to the duties of your Station. |
| | J Q W | Return to your Station. |

# PART V.

## SENTENCES.

### No Distinguishing Flag.

| Leading Words. | Letters. | S |
|---|---|---|
| Station. | J R B | Provided there are a sufficient number at the Station. |
| | J R C | There are a sufficient number at the Station. |
| | J R D | There are not a sufficient number at the Station. |
| Station Buoy. | J R F | Buoy Station. |
| | J R G | Take the Buoy Station. |
| | J R H | Do not take the Buoy Station. |
| | J R K | Will you take the Buoy Station? |
| | J R L | I will take the Buoy Station. |
| | J R M | I cannot take the Buoy Station. |
| | J R N | What Vessel is at the Buoy Station? |
| | J R P | *Vessel indicated* is at the Buoy Station. |
| | J R Q | There is no Vessel at the Buoy Station. |
| | J R S | Where is the Buoy Station Vessel? |
| | J R T | I will do the Buoy Station duties in your absence. |
| | J R V | Will you take the Buoy Station duties till I return from the duty ordered on? |
| | J R W | What Vessel is to relieve me from the Buoy Station? |

# PART V.

## SENTENCES.

### No Distinguishing Flag.

| Leading Words. | Letters. | S |
|---|---|---|
| **Station Buoy.** | J S B | *Vessel indicated* will relieve you from the Buoy Station. |
| | J S C | Vessel Buoy Station. |
| | J S D | Take the Buoy Station during my absence. |
| | J S F | Take the Buoy Station during absence of *Vessel indicated.* |
| | J S G | I have not supplies of Stores public to keep the Buoy Station. |
| | J S H | I have not supplies of Stores private to keep the Buoy Station. |
| | J S K | I have not supplies of Stores private beyond *date indicated* to keep the Buoy Station. |
| **Station Cruizing.** | J S L | Cruizing Station. |
| | J S M | Cruizing Station Vessel. |
| | J S N | Are you going to the Cruizing Station? |
| | J S P | I am going to the Cruizing Station. |
| | J S Q | I am not going to the Cruizing Station. |
| | J S R | Proceed to the Cruizing Station. |
| | J S T | What Vessel is at the Cruizing Station? |
| | J S V | Take the Cruizing Station. |
| | J S W | I have not supplies of Stores public to keep the Cruizing Station. |

| Leading Words. | Letters. | S |
|---|---|---|
| Station Cruizing. | J T B | I have not supplies of Stores private to keep the Cruizing Station. |
| | J T C | I have not supplies of Stores private beyond *date indicated* to keep the Cruizing Station. |
| Station Intermediate. | J T D | Intermediate Station. |
| | J T F | Intermediate Station Vessel. |
| | J T G | Take the Intermediate Station. |
| | J T H | I have not supplies of Stores public to keep the Intermediate Station. |
| | J T K | I have not supplies of Stores private to keep the Intermediate Station. |
| Steam. | J T L | Are you in want of Steam ? |
| | J T M | I am in want of Steam. |
| | J T N | I am not in want of Steam. |
| | J T P | Report I am in want of Steam. |
| | J T Q | I am waiting for a Steamer. |
| | J T R | A Steamer is coming down to you. |
| | J T S | No Steamer procurable. |
| | J T V | I am in distress—send your Steamer. |
| Steam Tug. | J T W | Is your Commander agreeable to share half the expense of a Steam Tug ? |

# PART V.

## SENTENCES.

### No Distinguishing Flag.

| LEADING WORDS. | LETTERS. | S |
|---|---|---|
| **Steam Tug.** | J V B | The Commander is agreeable to share half the expense of a Steam Tug. |
| | J V C | The Commander objects to share half the expense of a Steam Tug. |
| | J V D | *Vessel indicated* is in want of a Steam Tug at *place indicated*. |
| | J V F | Are there any Vessels in want of Steam Tugs ? |
| | J V G | There are Vessels in want of Steam Tugs. |
| | J V H | There are no Vessels in want of Steam Tugs. |
| **Steamer.** | J V K | Her Majesty's War Steamer. |
| | J V L | Her Majesty's Transport Steamer. |
| | J V M | Her Majesty's British Mail Steamer. |
| | J V N | Her Majesty's China Mail Steamer. |
| | J V P | Her Majesty's East Coast Mail Steamer. |
| | J V Q | Her Majesty's West Coast Mail Steamer. |
| | J V R | French Mail Steamer. |
| **Stock.** | J V S | Are you in want of Stock ? |
| | J V T | Can you spare me any Stock ? |
| | J V W | I can spare you some Stock. |

# PART V.

## SENTENCES.

### No Distinguishing Flag.

| LEADING WORDS. | LETTERS. | S |
|---|---|---|
| Stock. | J W B | I cannot spare you any Stock. |
| | J W C | May I proceed in for Stock ? |
| | J W D | I am going in for Stock. |
| | J W F | Shall I bring you some Stock ? |
| | J W G | Will you bring me *quantity indicated ?* |
| | J W H | How much Stock do you require ? |
| | J W K | Will you direct Stock to be sent down ? |
| | J W L | Will you ask *Officer indicated* to bring down Stock for me *quantity indicated?* |
| | J W M | I have Stock on board for you. |
| | J W N | *Vessel indicated* is bringing down Stock for you. |
| | J W P | No Stock procurable. |
| Stores. | J W Q | Send for your Stores. |
| | J W R | I will send your Stores by the first opportunity. |
| | J W S | *Vessel indicated* has private Stores for you. |
| | J W T | *Vessel indicated* has public Stores for you. |
| | J W V | Have you any Stores for me ? |

# PART V.

## SENTENCES.

### No Distinguishing Flag.

| LEADING WORDS. | LETTERS. | S |
|---|---|---|
| Stores. | K B C | I have public Stores for you on *Vessel indicated*. |
| | K B D | I have private Stores for you on *Vessel indicated*. |
| | K B F | In want of public Stores. |
| | K B G | In want of private Stores. |
| | K B H | There are public Stores on board of *Vessel indicated* for you. |
| | K B J | There are private Stores on board of *Vessel indicated* for you. |
| Sunk. | K B L | A Vessel has sunk off *place indicated* in the Channel. |
| | K B M | A Vessel has sunk off *place indicated* not in the Channel. |
| Supplies. | K B N | For what time have you Supplies ? |
| | K B P | Have Supplies to *date indicated*. |
| | K B Q | My Supplies are running short. |
| Survey. | K B R | Send your boat for Survey of *place indicated*. |
| | K B S | I will send you the Survey of *place indicated*. |
| Surveyor. | K B T | Come on board and see progress of Surveyor. |
| | K B V | Surveyor reports there is No. of feet reduced at *place indicated*. |
| | K B W | You had better place yourself in communication with the Surveyor for the information you require. |

*Faraday.*

# PART V.

## SENTENCES.

### No Distinguishing Flag.

| Leading Words. | Letters. | S |
|---|---|---|
| Surveyor. | K C B | Where is the Surveyor ? |
|  | K C D | Surveyor is at *place indicated*. |
|  | K C F | *Sunday.* |
|  | K C G |  |
|  | K C H |  |
|  | K C J |  |
|  | K C L |  |

# PART V.

## SENTENCES.

### No Distinguishing Flag.

| Leading Words. | Letters. | T |
|---|---|---|
| Tack. | K C M | Do not tack. |
| | K C N | I shall tack at *time indicated*. |
| | K C P | When I have tacked. |
| | K C Q | Signalize *Vessel indicated* to tack. |
| Thanks. | K C R | Thank you. |
| | K C S | Many thanks. |
| | K C T | Many thanks *for indicated*. |
| Tide. | K C V | At what time of tide ? |
| | K C W | At high water. |

*Third*
*Tenth.*
*Twentieth*
*Thirteenth*
*Thirty first*
*Twelfth*
*Twenty First*
*„ Second*
*„ Third*
*„ Fourth*
*„ Fifth*
*„ Sixth*
*„ Seventh.*
*„ Eighth*
*„ Ninth*

## SENTENCES.

### No Distinguishing Flag.

| Leading Words. | Letters. | T |
|---|---|---|
| Tide. | K D B | At low water. |
| | K D C | At first quarter flood. |
| | K D F | At half flood. |
| | K D G | At three quarters flood. |
| | K D H | At first quarter ebb. |
| | K D J | At half ebb. |
| | K D L | At three quarters ebb. |
| | K D M | On the flood. |
| | K D N | On the ebb. |
| | K D P | When the tide serves. |
| | K D Q | At slack water. |
| | K D R | What will tide rise to at *place indicated* to-day? |
| | K D S | Tide will or ought to rise to *feet indicated* to-day. |
| | K D T | What will tide fall to at *place indicated* to-day? |
| | K D V | Tide will or ought to fall to *feet indicated* to-day. |
| Tow. | K D W | Take me in tow when I swing. |

## SENTENCES.

### No Distinguishing Flag.

| Leading Words. | Letters. | T |
|---|---|---|
| Tow. | K F B | Take me in tow—the Vessel is in distress. |
| | K F C | Shall I take you in tow ? |
| Town. | K F D | Can I do anything for you in Town ? |
| | K F G | Report in Town all is well. |
| Track. | K F H | Take the usual Track. |
| | K F J | The best Track is *as indicated.* |
| | K F L | Go to Northward of usual Track. |
| | K F M | Go to Southward of usual Track. |
| | K F N | Go to Eastward of usual Track. |
| | K F P | Go to Westward of usual Track. |
| | K F Q | *Tuesday Thursday* |
| | K F R | *Tuesday.* |
| | K F S | |
| | K F T | |
| | K F V | |
| | K F W | |

# PART V.

## SENTENCES.

### No Distinguishing Flag.

| Leading Words. | Letters. | V |
|---|---|---|
| Vessel. | K G B | Vessel with Troops. |
| | K G C | Vessel with Emigrants. |
| | K G D | Vessel with Horses. |
| | K G F | Vessel with Elephants. |
| | K G H | Vessel with Bullocks. |
| | K G J | Vessel with Convicts. |
| | K G L | Vessel with Pilgrims. |
| | K G M | Vessel with Camels. |
| | K G N | Vessel with Mules. |
| | K G P | Vessel with Steam. |
| | K G Q | Vessel in Tow. |
| | K G R | Vessel adrift bearing *as indicated*. |
| | K G S | Vessel without rudder bearing *as indicated*. |
| | K G T | Vessel without anchors bearing *as indicated*. |
| | K G V | Vessel without masts bearing *as indicated*. |
| | K G W | Vessel with jury masts bearing *as indicated*. |

# PART V.

## SENTENCES.

### No Distinguishing Flag.

| LEADING WORDS. | LETTERS. | V |
|---|---|---|
| Vessel. | K H B | Vessel on fire bearing *as indicated*. |
| | K H C | Vessel in distress bearing *as indicated*. |
| | K H D | Vessel reported at *place indicated*—proceed and look for her. |
| | K H F | Vessel in sight bearing *as indicated*. |
| | K H G | Of what Nation is the Vessel ? |
| | K H J | Of what description is the Vessel ? |
| | K H L | I cannot make out the Vessel. |
| | K H M | Vessel in sight looks suspicious. |
| | K H N | Vessel in sight is an Enemy. |
| | K H P | Vessel in sight is a Friend. |
| | K H Q | Vessel in sight is H. M.'s |
| | K H R | Vessel in sight is British. |
| | K H S | Vessel in sight is French. |
| | K H T | Vessel in sight is American. |
| | K H V | Vessel in sight is Russian. |
| | K H W | Vessel in sight is Prussian. |

# PART V.

## SENTENCES.

### No Distinguishing Flag.

| Leading Words. | Letters. | V |
|---|---|---|
| Vessel. | K J B | Vessel in sight is Danish. |
| | K J C | Vessel in sight is Sardinian. |
| | K J D | Vessel in sight is Portuguese. |
| | K J F | Vessel in sight is Chinese. |
| | K J G | Vessel in sight is Genoese. |
| | K J H | Vessel in sight is Arabian. |
| | K J L | Vessel in sight is Coaster. |
| | K J M | Vessel in sight is an Outward Steamer. |
| | K J N | Vessel in sight is an Inward Steamer. |
| | K J P | How many Outward-bound Vessels are there below Saugor ? |
| | K J Q | What Vessels have passed out ? |
| | K J R | What Vessels have passed in ? |
| | K J S | Vessel *indicated* has passed out. |
| | K J T | Vessel *indicated* has passed in. |
| | K J V | Vessel *indicated* is missing. |
| | K J W | |

# PART V.

## SENTENCES.

### No Distinguishing Flag.

| LEADING WORDS. | LETTERS. | V |
|---|---|---|
| | K L B | |
| | K L C | |
| | K L D | |
| | K L F | |

# PART V.

## SENTENCES.

### No Distinguishing Flag.

| Leading Words. | Letters. | W |
|---|---|---|
| Wait. | K L G | Shall I wait ? |
| | K L H | Do not wait. |
| | K L J | I cannot wait. |
| | K L M | Wait till *time indicated*. |
| | K L N | You must wait. |
| Want. | K L P | Are you in want of any thing ? |
| | K L Q | I am in want of *as indicated*. |
| | K L R | I am not in want of anything. |
| Water. | K L S | I am in want of Water. |
| | K L T | I am not in want of Water. |
| | K L V | *Vessel indicated* is in want of Water. |
| | K L W | *Vessel indicated* is coming down with Water. |

# PART V.

## SENTENCES.

### No Distinguishing Flag.

| Leading Words. | Letters. | W |
|---|---|---|
| Water. | K M B | Will you supply me or *Vessel indicated* with Water. |
| | K M C | I will supply you or *Vessel indicated* with Water. |
| | K M D | I cannot supply you or *Vessel indicated* with Water. |
| | K M F | Supply *Vessel indicated* with Water. |
| | K M G | What quantity of Water have you on board? |
| | K M H | I have on board No. of gallons *indicated.* |
| | K M J | I have only enough Water for my own use. |
| | K M L | Shall I have sufficient Water through Channel *indicated* or over Bar *indicated?* |
| | K M N | You will have sufficient Water through Channel *indicated* or over Bar *indicated.* |
| | K M P | You will not have sufficient Water through Channel *indicated* or over Bar *indicated.* |
| | K M Q | Show me the Water through Channel *indicated* or over Bar *indicated.* |
| Wear. | K M R | I shall wear. |
| | K M S | Do not wear. |
| | K M T | I am going to wear. |
| | K M V | Is there room to wear? |
| | K M W | There is room to wear. |

# PART V.

## SENTENCES.

### No Distinguishing Flag.

| Leading Words. | Letters. | W |
|---|---|---|
| Wear. | K N B | There is not room to wear. |
| Weather. | K N C | What do you think of the appearance of the weather ? |
| | K N D | Weather looks unsettled. |
| | K N F | Weather looks suspicious. |
| | K N G | Weather looks alarming. |
| | K N H | When the weather moderates. |
| | K N J | Should the weather be favorable. |
| | K N L | Should the weather be unfavorable. |
| | K N M | Should the weather continue as it is shall go to sea. |
| | K N P | Should the weather get worse shall go to sea. |
| | K N Q | Signalize to Vessels weather is getting unsettled to go to sea. |
| | K N R | Signalize to Vessels weather is getting unsettled to be prepared to go to sea and for bad weather. |
| | K N S | Signalize to Vessels to go to sea without any delay as weather and Barometer indicate a gale. |
| Weigh. | K N T | Shall I weigh ? |
| | K N V | Signalize all Vessels to weigh. |
| | K N W | Signalize Vessel or *Vessels indicated* to weigh. |
| | | *Wednesday* |

# PART V.

## SENTENCES.

### No Distinguishing Flag.

| LEADING WORDS. | LETTERS. | W |
|---|---|---|
| Weigh. | K P B | When shall I weigh ? |
| | K P C | Weigh now or at *time indicated*. |
| | K P D | Weigh when wind changes to *quarter indicated*. |
| | K P F | Weigh at high water. |
| | K P G | Weigh at low water. |
| | K P H | Weigh when sea goes down. |
| | K P J | Weigh at once. |
| | K P L | When will you weigh ? |
| | K P M | I shall weigh now or at *time indicated*. |
| | K P N | I shall weigh when wind changes to *quarter indicated*. |
| | K P Q | I shall weigh at high water. |
| | K P R | I shall weigh at low water. |
| | K P S | I shall weigh at once. |
| | K P T | I shall weigh when sea goes down. |
| | K P V | I shall weigh when weather moderates. |
| | K P W | I shall weigh when weather gets settled. |

# PART V.

## SENTENCES.

### No Distinguishing Flag.

| LEADING WORDS. | LETTERS. | W |
|---|---|---|
| Weigh. | K Q B | Signalize Vessels that cannot weigh their anchors to slip and go to Sea without any delay. |
| Well. | K Q C | All is well. |
| | K Q D | All are not well. |
| | K Q F | We are all well. |
| | K Q G | I hope you are all well. |
| Windlass. | K Q H | My windlass is injured—I cannot weigh. |
| | K Q J | My windlass is injured and cannot be repaired. |
| | K Q L | My windlass is injured and can be repaired. |
| Windwand. | K Q M | Work to windward. |
| | K Q N | Work to windward till tide turns. |
| | K Q P | I shall work to windward till tide turns. |
| Writing. | K Q R | Write and report the circumstance. |
| | K Q S | I have reported the circumstance by writing. |
| | K Q T | I shall write and report the circumstance. |
| | K Q V | Have you reported the circumstance by writing ? |
| | K Q W | I have not reported the circumstance by writing. |
| | | *Windlass purchase is carried away.* |

## SENTENCES.

### No Distinguishing Flag.

| LEADING WORDS. | LETTERS. | W |
|---|---|---|
| Wreck. | K R B | *Vessel indicated* wrecked on or at *place indicated.* |
| | K R C | There is a wreck on or at *place indicated.* |
| | K R D | There is a wreck reported on or at *place indicated.* |
| | K R F | A wreck in sight bearing and distance *as indicated.* |
| | K R G | Have you heard of the wreck of *Vessel indicated ?* |
| | K R H | |
| | K R J | |
| | K R L | |
| | K R M | |
| | K R N | |

# PART V.

## SENTENCES.

### No Distinguishing Flag.

| LEADING WORDS. | LETTERS. | Y |
|---|---|---|
| Yard. | K R P | Yard main. |
| | K R Q | Yard main-topsail upper. |
| | K R S | Yard main-topsail lower. |
| | K R T | Yard main-topgallant. |
| | K R V | Yard main-royal. |
| | K R W | Yard, fore. |

# PART V.

—

## SENTENCES.

### No Distinguishing Flag.

| LEADING WORDS. | LETTERS. | Y |
|---|---|---|
| Yard. | K S B | Yard fore-top-sail upper. |
| | K S C | Yard fore-top-sail lower. |
| | K S D | Yard fore-top-sail gallant. |
| | K S F | Yard fore-royal. |
| Yesterday. | K S G | Yesterday morning *hour indicated*. |
| | K S H | Yesterday afternoon *hour indicated*. |
| | K S J | Yesterday noon. |
| | K S L | Yesterday. |
| | K S M | |
| | K S N | |
| | K S P | |
| | K S Q | |
| | K S R | |

## RIVER SURVEYOR'S SIGNALS.

### Telegraph Flag over Letter.

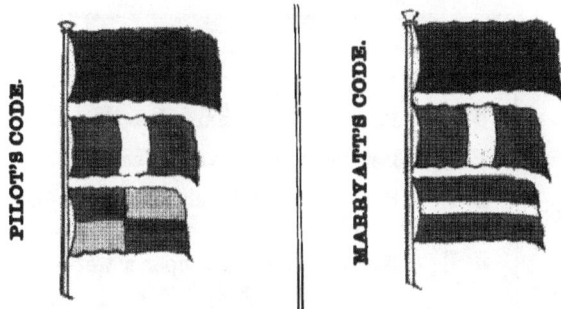

There is anchorage off Buoy or place (indicated) feet reduced (indicated).

| Leading Words. | Letters. | **A** |
|---|---|---|
| **Altera-tions.** | **B** | Alterations have been made in position of Buoy *indicated* in Channel *indicated*. |
| | **C** | |
| | **D** | |
| | **F** | |
| | **G** | |
| **Anchorage.** | **H** | There is anchorage off Buoy or *place indicated* feet reduced *indicated*. |
| | **J** | |
| | **K** | |
| | **L** | |
| | **M** | |
| | **N** | |
| | **P** | |
| | **R** | |
| | **T** | |
| | **V** | |
| | **W** | |

# PART V.

## RIVER SURVEYOR'S SIGNALS.

### Telegraph Flag over Letter.

| Leading Words. | Letters. | B |
|---|---|---|
| Bar. | B C | Bar Upper of Channel *indicated*. |
| | B D | Bar Lower of Channel *indicated*. |
| | B F | Bar *indicated* is shoal water—will be shown in *feet reduced*. |
| | B G | Bar *indicated* is deeper water—will be shown in *feet reduced*. |
| | B H | Bar has formed in Channel *indicated* about Buoy or *position indicated*—least water shown in *feet reduced*. |
| Boat. | B J | Look out for boat with information in Channel *indicated* or off *place indicated*. |
| | B K | Boat showing Flag *indicated* is anchored on Shoal or Lump *indicated*. |
| | B L | |
| | B M | Boat showing Flag *indicated* is anchored in best track Channel Bar or *place indicated*. |
| | B N | |
| | B P | |
| | B Q | |
| | B R | |
| | B T | |
| | B V | |
| | B W | |

# PART V.

## RIVER SURVEYOR'S SIGNALS.

### Telegraph Flag over Letter.

| Leading Words. | Letters. | C |
|---|---|---|
| Changes. | C B | Changes *as indicated* have been made in Buoys in Channel *indicated*. |
| | C D | Changes have occurred in Channel *indicated*. |
| | C F | |
| | C G | |
| | C H | |
| Channel. | C J | Channel *indicated* is open and buoyed. |
| | C K | Channel *indicated* is closed. |
| | C L | Keep mid Channel *indicated*. |
| | C M | |
| | C N | |
| Communicate. | C P | Communicate with Surveying Vessel in Channel or off *place indicated*. |
| | C Q | |
| | C R | |
| | C T | |
| Colour. | C V | Red. |
| | C W | Black. |

## RIVER SURVEYOR'S SIGNALS.

### Telegraph Flag over Letter.

| LEADING WORDS. | LETTERS. | C |
|---|---|---|
| Colour. | D B | Blue. |
| | D C | White. |
| | D F | Green. |
| | D G | Yellow. |
| | D H | Black and White. |
| | D J | Red and White. |
| | D K | Blue and White. |
| | D L | |
| | D M | |
| | D N | |
| | D P | |
| | D Q | |
| | D R | |
| | D T | |
| | D V | |
| | D W | |

## RIVER SURVEYOR'S SIGNALS.

### Telegraph Flag over Letter.

| Leading Words. | Letters. | E |
|---|---|---|
| | G B | |
| | C C | |
| Ease. | C D | Heave to or ease speed for Boat or Row Boat with communication from River Surveyor in Channel *indicated.* |
| | C F | |
| | G H | |
| | G J | |
| | G K | |
| | C L | Keep on Eastern side of Channel. |
| | C M | |
| | C N | Pass to Eastward of Buoy *indicated* in Channel *indicated.* |
| | G P | |
| | G Q | |
| | G R | |
| | C T | |
| | C V | |
| | G W | |

# PART V.

## RIVER SURVEYOR'S SIGNALS.

### Telegraph Flag over Letter.

| LEADING WORDS. | LETTERS. | L |
|---|---|---|
| Lump. | H B | Lump has formed in Channel *indicated* near Buoy or *place indicated* with soundings on it *as indicated*. |
| | H C | |
| | H D | Pass to Eastward of Lump. |
| | H F | Pass to Westward of Lump. |
| | H G | Nun Buoy has been laid on Lump *indicated*. |
| | H J | Lump *indicated* has disappeared. |
| | H K | Lump *indicated* has extended in *direction indicated* by Compass Signal. |
| | H L | |
| | H M | |
| | H N | |
| | H P | |
| | H Q | |
| | H R | |

# PART V.

## RIVER SURVEYOR'S SIGNALS.

### Telegraph Flag over Letter.

| LEADING WORDS. | LETTERS. | S |
|---|---|---|
| Shoal. | H T | There is shoal water *feet indicated* in or near *place indicated.* |
| | H V | |
| | H W | There is shoal water to Eastward of Buoy or *place indicated.* |

# PART V.

## RIVER SURVEYOR'S SIGNALS.

### Telegraph Flag over Letter.

| LEADING WORDS. | LETTERS. | S |
|---|---|---|
| | J B | |
| Shoal. | J C | There is shoal water to Westward of Buoy or *place indicated.* |
| | J D | |
| | J F | There is shoal water bearing as per Compass *indicated* from object *indicated.* |
| | J G | |
| | J H | |
| | J K | |
| | J L | |
| | J M | |
| | J N | |

# PART V.

## RIVER SURVEYOR'S SIGNALS.

### Telegraph Flag over Letter.

| LEADING WORDS. | LETTERS. | T |
|---|---|---|
| Track. | J P | Best track over *place indicated* is feet reduced in *Marryatt's Numerals*. |
| | J Q | |
| | J R | Easterly. |
| | J T | Westerly. |
| Transit. | J V | Line of transit Buoy or object *indicated* on Buoy or object *indicated*. |
| | J W | |

# PART V.

## RIVER SURVEYOR'S SIGNALS.

### Telegraph Flag over Letter.

| Leading Words. | Letters. | T |
|---|---|---|
| Track. | **K B** | Buoy or object *indicated* open to East-ward of object *indicated*. |
| | **K C** | |
| | **K D** | Buoy or object *indicated* open to West-ward of object *indicated*. |
| | **K F** | |
| | **K G** | Buoy or object *indicated* midway be-tween object *indicated*. |
| | **K H** | |
| | **K J** | Tracks *indicated* have shoaled; least water shown in feet by *Marryatt's Numerals*. |
| | **K L** | |
| | **K M** | Tracks *indicated* have deepened; least water shown in feet by *Marryatt's Numerals*. |
| | **K N** | |
| | **K P** | Track over Bar *indicated* is *as indicated*. |
| | **K Q** | |
| | **K R** | |
| | **K T** | |
| | **K V** | |
| | **K W** | |

# PART V.

## RIVER SURVEYOR'S SIGNALS.

### Telegraph Flag over Letter.

| Leading Words. | Letters. | W |
|---|---|---|
| | **L B** | Keep on Western side of Channel *indicated*. |
| Westward. | **L C** | Pass to Westward of Buoy *indicated* in Channel *indicated*. |
| | **L D** | |
| | **L F** | |
| | **L G** | |
| | **L H** | |
| | **L J** | |
| Wreck. | **L K** | There is a wreck in Channel *indicated*. |
| | **L M** | Pass to Eastward of wreck in Channel *indicated*. |
| | **L N** | Pass to Westward of wreck in Channel *indicated*. |
| | **L P** | Pass to Northward of wreck in Channel *indicated*. |
| | **L Q** | Pass to Southward of wreck in Channel *indicated*. |
| | **L R** | Wreck Buoy has been laid *as indicated*. |
| | **L T** | Wreck Buoy *as indicated* is adrift. |
| | **L V** | |
| | **L W** | |

# PART V.

## RIVER SURVEYOR'S SIGNALS.

### Telegraph Flag over Letter.

| Leading Words. | Letters. | W |
|---|---|---|
| | M B | |
| | M C | |
| | M D | |

# PART VI.

## COMPASS SIGNALS.

Distinguished by White Flag over Letter.

# PART VI.

## COMPASS SIGNALS.

### White Flag over Letter.

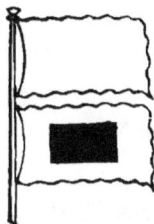

PILOT'S CODE.

N W by N.

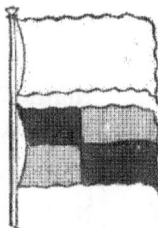

MARRYATT'S CODE.

N W by N.

| LETTERS. | POINTS OF COMPASS. |
|---|---|
| B | North. |
| C | North quarter West. |
| D | North half West. |
| F | North three quarters West. |
| G | North by West. |
| H | North by West quarter West. |
| J | North by West half West. |
| K | North by West three quarters West. |
| L | North-North-West. |
| M | North-North-West quarter West. |
| N | North-North-West half West. |
| P | North-North-West three quarters West. |
| Q | North-West by North. |
| R | North-West by North quarter West. |
| S | North-West by North half West. |
| T | North-West by North three quarters West. |
| V | North-West. |
| W | North-West quarter West. |

# PART VI.

## COMPASS SIGNALS.

### White Flag over Letter.

| LETTERS. | POINTS OF COMPASS. |
| --- | --- |
| B C | North-West half West. |
| B D | North-West three quarters West. |
| B F | North-West by West. |
| B G | North-West by West quarter West. |
| B H | North-West by West half West. |
| B J | North-West by West three quarters West. |
| B K | West-North-West. |
| B L | West. |
| B M | West quarter North. |
| B N | West half North. |
| B P | West three quarters North. |
| B Q | West by North. |
| B R | West by North quarter North. |
| B S | West by North half North. |
| B T | West by North three quarters North. |
| B V | South quarter West. |
| B W | South half West. |

# PART VI.

## COMPASS SIGNALS.

### White Flag over Letter.

| LETTERS. | POINTS OF COMPASS. |
|---|---|
| C B | South quarter West. |
| C D | South half West. |
| C F | South three quarters West. |
| C G | South by West. |
| C H | South by West quarter West. |
| C J | South by West half West. |
| C K | South by West three quarters West. |
| C L | South-South-West. |
| C M | South-South-West quarter West. |
| C N | South-South-West half West. |
| C P | South-South-West three quarters West. |
| C Q | South-West by South. |
| C R | South-West by South quarter West. |
| C S | South-West by South half West. |
| C T | South-West by South three quarters West. |
| C V | South-West. |
| C W | South-West quarter West. |

# PART VI.

## COMPASS SIGNALS.

### White Flag over Letter.

| LETTERS. | POINTS OF COMPASS. |
|---|---|
| D B | South-West half West. |
| D C | South-West three quarters West. |
| D F | South-West by West. |
| D G | South-West by West quarter West. |
| D H | South-West by West half West. |
| D J | South-West by West three quarters West. |
| D K | West-South-West. |
| D L | West quarter South. |
| D M | West half South. |
| D N | West three quarters South. |
| D P | West by South. |
| D Q | West by South quarter South. |
| D R | West by South half South. |
| D S | West by South three quarters South. |
| D T | North quarter East. |
| D V | North half East. |
| D W | North three quarters East. |

## COMPASS SIGNALS.

### White Flag over Letter.

| Letters. | Points of Compass. |
|---|---|
| F B | North by East. |
| F C | North by East quarter East. |
| F D | North by East half East. |
| F G | North by East three quarters East. |
| F H | North-North-East. |
| F J | North-North-East quarter East. |
| F K | North-North-East half East. |
| F L | North-North-East three quarters East. |
| F M | North-East by North. |
| F N | North-East by North quarter East. |
| F P | North-East by North half East. |
| F Q | North-East by North three quarters East. |
| F R | North-East. |
| F S | North-East quarter East. |
| F T | North-East half East. |
| F V | North-East three quarters East. |
| F W | North-East by East. |

# PART VI.

## COMPASS SIGNALS.

### White Flag over Letter.

| LETTERS. | POINTS OF COMPASS. |
|---|---|
| G B | North-East by East quarter East. |
| G C | North-East by East half East. |
| G D | North-East by East three quarters East. |
| G F | East-North-East. |
| G H | East. |
| G J | East quarter North. |
| G K | East half North. |
| G L | East three quarters North. |
| G M | East by North. |
| G N | East by North quarter North. |
| G P | East by North half North. |
| G Q | East by North three quarters North. |
| G R | South. |
| G S | South quarter East. |
| G T | South half East. |
| G V | South three quarters East. |
| G W | South by East. |

# PART VI.

## COMPASS SIGNALS.

### White Flag over Letter.

| Letters. | Points of Compass. |
|---|---|
| H B | South by East quarter East. |
| H C | South by East half East. |
| H D | South by East three quarters East. |
| H F | South-South-East. |
| H G | South-South-East quarter East. |
| H J | South-South-East half East. |
| H K | South-South-East three quarters East. |
| H L | South-East by South. |
| H M | South-East by South quarter East. |
| H N | South-East by South half East. |
| H P | South-East by South three quarters East. |
| H Q | South-East. |
| H R | South-East quarter East. |
| H S | South-East half East. |
| H T | South-East three quarters East. |
| H V | South-East by East. |
| H W | South-East by East quarter East. |

# PART IV.

## COMPASS SIGNALS.

### White Flag over Letter.

| Letters. | Points of Compass. |
|---|---|
| J B | South-East by East half East. |
| J C | South-East by East three quarter East. |
| J D | East-South-East. |
| J F | East quarter South. |
| J G | East half South. |
| J H | East three quarters South. |
| J K | East by South. |
| J L | East by South quarter South. |
| J M | East by South half South. |
| J N | East by South three quarters South. |

# PART VII.

## NIGHT SIGNALS.

# PART VII.

## NIGHT SIGNALS.

| LANTNS BY THEM-SELVES. | SIGNIFICATIONS. |
| --- | --- |
| | Send me a Boat. |
| | I will join you from the Steamer. |
| | I will take you out at day-light. |
| | Anchor. |
| | Weigh. |
| | Come within hail. |
| | I will take you out now. |
| | Lay to on the Starboard Tack. |
| | Lay to on the Portack. |

*Note.*—Night Signals to be answered by a single Light, or if a Light be up by a Maroon; a "Blue Light" singly is affirmative, a "Gun" is negative.
When Night Signals are shown a space of three feet is to be kept between the Lanterns.

| LANTERNS SHOWN WITH A "MAROON." | SIGNIFICATIONS. |
|---|---|
| | My Boat is capsized; try to save t' ' w |
| | You must come on board in your own Boat, mine not being in a fit state to send away. |
| | Beat to Windward till turn of Tide. |
| | There are Vessels following in want of Pilots. |
| | I have no Officers on board. |
| | I come for Officers. |
| | False Point. |
| | False Bay. |
| | Point Palmiras. |

# PART VII.

## NIGHT SIGNALS.

Balasore Roads.

Western Brace.

Kel or Kiln.

Western Reef.

Western Channel.

Eastern Reef.

Eastern Channel.

Saugor Sand.

Lacam's Channel.

www.ingramcontent.com/pod-product-compliance
Lightning Source LLC
Chambersburg PA
CBHW020509270326
41926CB00008B/808